American School of Prehistoric Research

Peabody Museum • Harvard University
Bulletin 39

The Proto-Elamite Texts from Tepe Yahya

Peter Damerow

Max Planck Institute for Human Development and Education, Berlin

Robert K. Englund

Department of Near Eastern Archaeology, Free University of Berlin

With an introduction by
C. C. Lamberg-Karlovsky

Peabody Museum of Archaeology and Ethnology

PEABODY MUSEUM OF ARCHAEOLOGY AND ETHNOLOGY
Harvard University, Cambridge, Massachusetts
1989

Preface to Second Printing

Late in 1986 the three of us agreed to study the fairly unassuming collection of twenty-six proto-elamite tablets from the Harvard excavations of Tepe Yahya in southern Persia. As we learned, big surprises often come in small packages. While the Yahya texts did not compete, in complexity or content, with the very substantial corpus from the contemporaneous urban center at Susa, their analysis forced us to review the earlier philological and archaeological efforts expended on the proto-elamite phase of the ancient Near East (ca. 3100–2900 B.C.). Our objective was to produce a readable update of a field of scholarship that was, for the most part, lost on all but a few specialists. Our edition of the Yahya corpus was printed in 1989. That the Peabody Museum Press has decided to offer here an unaltered second printing of the original is testimony, first, to the sad fact that the events in Iran and Iraq have kept archaeological investigations of ancient Persia in a state of suspended animation for now over twenty years and, second, to our belief that its textual analysis represents a level of interpretation as applicable today as it was when we first had the pleasure of offering it.

Peter Damerow
Robert K. Englund
C. C. Lamberg-Karlovsky
May 2003

Copyright 1989 by the President and Fellows of Harvard College
ISBN 0-87365-542-7
Library of Congress Catalog Card Number 89-61400
Printed in the Federal Republic of Germany
Second Printing 2003

Contents

Figures

INTRODUCTION

The excavations at Tepe Yahya were undertaken in the summer months of 1968-71, 1973 and 1975. The first volume detailing *The Early Periods*, *ca. 5000-3500 B.C.*, has recently been published (Lamberg-Karlovsky and Beale 1986). The excavations were principally financed by the National Science Foundation, the Ford Foundation, and private benefactors. The Tepe Yahya Project was sponsored by the Peabody Museum of Archaeology and Ethnology, Harvard University, and the Archaeological Service of the Ministry of Culture of Iran.

In the summer of 1970, within our main step trench, we exposed, for the first time, what we referred to as Period IVC. In a small test trench within Area B (see Lamberg-Karlovsky and Beale 1968, Chapter 2, for the periodization, geographical setting, and description of the site), we uncovered a portion of a large building which contained proto-elamite tablets, tablet blanks, cylinder sealings, beveled-rim bowls, and biconical-lugged bichrome ceramics. The six proto-elamite tablets recovered in that first season were published in *Kadmos* (Lamberg-Karlovsky 1971). The significant results of the 1970 season were published in an article in *Iran* (Lamberg-Karlovsky 1971b). For several years these remained the principal publications on the proto-elamite tablets from Tepe Yahya. Most of the tablets recovered in subsequent seasons from the Period IVC building were published in preliminary copy and without comment in Lamberg-Karlovsky and Tosi 1973 and Lamberg-Karlovsky 1976.

The excavation of the Period IVC proto-elamite building was undertaken in 1970 by Martha Prickett, Philip Kohl, and Nagaraja Rao; in 1971 by Martha Prickett, Elizabeth Stone, and Thomas Layton; in 1973 by Daniel Potts, Connie Piesinger, and Tom Beale; and in 1975 by Daniel Potts, Tom Beale, and Maurizio Tosi. The excavation of Period IVC entailed a horizontal exposure of almost 500 square meters. The architecture consisted of a single building complex, excavated within 10 x 10 meter squares within Areas A, B, BW, C, and CW. Two specialized studies have been published pertaining to this proto-elamite building. The first study undertook an analysis of the beveled-rim bowls from Tepe Yahya and attempted to test the hypothesis of their being standardized units of measure (Beale 1978). The second study was also undertaken by Beale (Beale and Carter 1983) and successfully proved that at Tepe Yahya the bricks conformed to a standardized unit of measurement, and, more importantly, that the entire building was laid out utilizing a standard unit of linear measurement. It is evident from Figure 1, which locates within the building the provenience of each of the 26 proto-elamite tablets (excluding the tablet published below as no. 27), that only a percentage of the building complex was uncovered. The large wall, recovered at the southeastern extremity at the contour of the mound, was cut by pit 12 (see Fig. 1) and poorly preserved. It is difficult to ascertain whether this wall represents another building, or, more likely, a circumvallation wall surrounding the IVC proto-elamite building.

In 1975, Professor Maurizio Tosi encouraged me to place the entire corpus of proto-elamite texts from Tepe Yahya at the disposal of Professor Piero Meriggi. The notable contributions made by Professor Meriggi (1971-74) to the study of proto-elamite made this a most welcome suggestion. The completed study of Professor Meriggi was to be published in a separate volume of contributions devoted to Period IVC. With more detailed study of this proto-elamite settlement, these studies became increasingly obsolete, and the entire project was abandoned in light of the forthcoming publication of a final volume detailing the entire third millennium corpus recovered from Tepe Yahya. In this forthcoming volume the seals and sealings from

Period IVC will be published by Dr. Holly Pittman of the Metropolitan Museum of Art and the ceramics by Dr. Daniel Potts of the Carsten Niebuhr Insitute, University of Copenhagen. It was Daniel Potts, as aptly described by the authors in this volume, who placed me in con tact with Dr. Peter Damerow and Dr. Robert Englund. Their on-going comprehensive study of the archaic texts from Mesopotamia and Susa provided the ideal background for an up-to-date analysis of the corpus from Tepe Yahya. It is a pleasure to acknowledge my gratitude to the authors of this monograph for their detailed analysis of the texts from Tepe Yahya. The earlier paper by Professor Meriggi on the Yahya texts will be published by Professor Giovanni Pettinato in *Oriens Antiquus*. It should be apparent, however, that the present publi- cation of the proto-elamite texts from Tepe Yahya supersedes all previous commentary on the nature of these tablets. An article based on the meanings of certain signs on the Yahya tablets, as identified by Professor Meriggi, was recently prepared by Maurizio Tosi and myself (in press). Although there are certain differences accorded the meaning of identical signs, as identified by Piero Meriggi, Peter Damerow, and Robert Englund, our basic analysis of the functions of the texts as economic accounts remains the same. A few brief comments on certain aspects, all of which will be detailed in more comprehensive fashion in the final publication on the third millennium at Tepe Yahya, are put forth below.

Chronology

Period IVC consists of two phases, an earlier IVC2 and a later IVC1. Within Figure 1 the walls depicted as solid black in the northeast quadrant are of the later IVC1 phases. The tablets in Area C of the building complex *may be* of a later date than those within the rooms of the building complex. The reason we say "*may be*" is due to the fact that we cannot provide a definitive judgment, for we could not trace the floor of Area C uniformly across the entire area - in too many places the floor was simply not evident. Tablets 22, 24, 25 and 26 did rest, however, on the floor upon which the blackened walls were constructed - these walls were constructed from a floor which was some 15 cm *above* the floor of the construction of the main building. These tablets (22; 24-26) are placed within Period IVC1 - tablets 12-13 and 16 rested on a floor which was impossible to trace as belonging to either the main building or its later phase. The excavator, nevertheless, felt they all belonged to Period IVC1, that is, the later phase. Within the rooms of the main building, in Room 5, the blank tablets and tablets 1- 6 and 8 rested *directly* upon the floor; in Room 1b tablets 9 and 10 rested upon the floor while tablet 7 was found in fill *ca.* 10 cm *above* the floor; in Room 1a, where eight tablets were found, tablets 17-21 were found directly on the floor, while tablets 11, 14, and 15 were found in fill directly above the floor. Thus, it is evident that while the majority of the tablets were found on the floors, a few were found in fill, while others belonged to a slightly later phase (IVC1) following the building's initial construction. Although it is exceedingly difficult to assess the duration of Period IVC, we do not believe that it was inhabited for longer than a century. It is important to recall that together with the tablets, cylinder sealings, ceramic storage vessels, a metal vessel containing natrojarosite (Reindell and Riederer 1979), a metal spear head, two large biconical heulandite beads, and an alabaster vessel are among some of the artifacts that were found resting directly upon the floors of the building. The abundant materials, seemingly of high value, left upon the floors of the building suggest a sudden abandonment of the building complex.

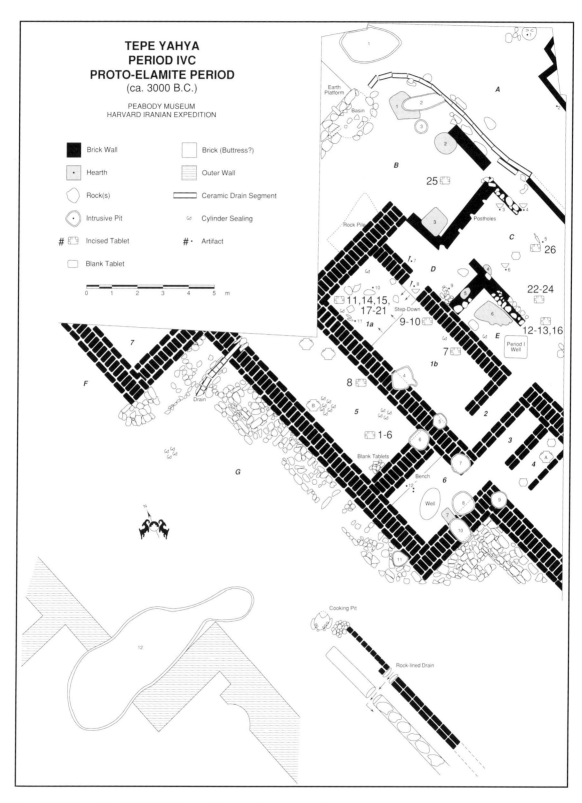

Figure 1. Plan of the IVC building at Tepe Yahya: tablet find locations.

Three radiocarbon dates, derived from charcoal samples, are available for Period IVC:

Lab No.	Locus	BP 55 68	Calibration	Calib. Midpoint
GX 5159	B20a 1970	4310 ± 195	4310 *200	2955 B.C.
		3485-2425 B.C.		
GX 5160	BW-CW7.7 1971	4150 ± 275	4150 *300	2790 B.C.
		3480-2100 B.C.		
TUNC 37	B.1 (1971)	4725 ± 115	4730 *100	3490 B.C.
		3780-3185		

The presence of beveled-rim bowls, numerous "Piedmont Style" cylinder sealing impressions and biconical-lugged vessels suggest a date contemporary with the Jemdet Nasr horizon of Mesopotamia, that is, within the last century of the fourth millennium.

Settlement pattern

At Tepe Yahya, Period IVC is unique in representing a settlement of short duration which is both preceded and followed by a gap in settlement continuity. It is, thus, a settlement "event," a community bearing little resemblance to the material culture which preceded and followed it. Settlement surveys, undertaken on behalf of the Yahya Project by Dr. Martha Prickett, indicate a dramatic abandonment of settlement regime prior to the establishment of Period IVC at Tepe Yahya. The Yahya IVC period saw the *total* abandonment of the nearby Shah Maran-Daulatabad basin, 25 kilometers from Tepe Yahya, where dozens of sites were occupied during the preceding Yahya Period VA (Prickett 1986). Similarly, there is a marked decrease in contemporary (late fourth millennium) settlement size and settlement number in the vicinity of Tal-i Iblis on the Bardsir plain. Settlement pattern studies indicate that prior to Period IVC there were numerous sites, of a regional nature, scattered throughout southeastern Iran from 5000 to 3500 B.C. In the earliest periods (Yahya VII-VI: 5000-4000 B.C.) archaeological sites were fewer in number but fairly large, up to 10 hectares. In the subsequent periods (Yahya VC-VA 4000-3300 B.C.) sites increased *substantially* in number but were rarely in excess of 1.5 hectares in size (for full documentation, see Prickett 1986). Toward the end of the fourth millennium these small and apparently self-sufficient agricultural communities experienced a crisis in their settlement regime; entire areas of dense settlement are wholly abandoned (Shah Maran-Daulatabad basin) while other areas experience a marked decrease in settlement size and number (Bardsir plain, Jiroft). Four aspects are of relevance concerning this settlement crisis and its aftermath:

1. An Aliabad Phase, identified at Tal-i Iblis, is hypothesized as representing continuous settlement through the presence of numerous small scattered sites throughout the region. These small sites, often of single period occupation, have been suggested by Martha Prickett as representing an increase in, or the development of, nomadism.

2. Contemporary with the Aliabad Phase, and following the settlement collapse, the proto-elamite community is established at Tepe Yahya. That it is not the only such settlement in eastern Iran is suggested by the presence of beveled-rim bowls at Tal-i Iblis (Caldwell 1967), a proto-elamite tablet and piedmont style cylinder sealings at Shahr-i Sokhta (Amiet

and Tosi 1978), and typologically similar ceramics and tablet blanks at Hissar (Dyson 1987).

3. Following the proto-elamite presence in eastern Iran, and seen most clearly at Tepe Yahya, there is little continuity in the material culture within the subsequent settlements. Written texts are not evident on the Iranian Plateau again for over a millennium, while ceramic and seal traditions bear little relationship to the earlier proto-elamite styles.

4. Following the abandonment of the proto-elamite settlements in eastern Iran, the third millennium is characterized by the emergence of regional urban centers, i.e., Shahr-i Sokhta, Shahdad, Hissar, and increasing interaction with Central Asia and Baluchistan.

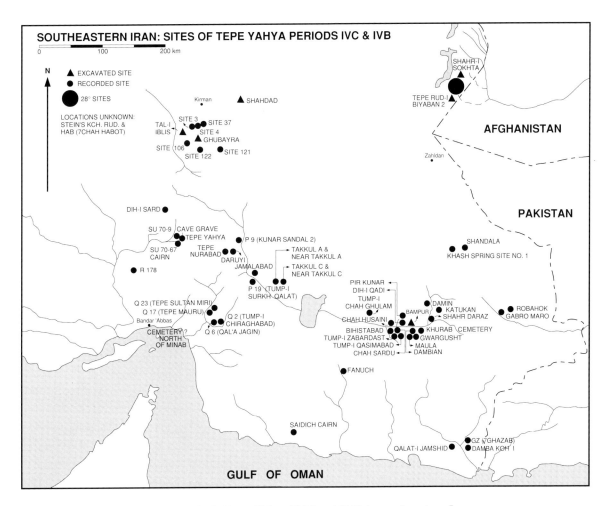

Figure 2. Map of sites in the periods Tepe Yahya IVC and IVB in southeastern Iran.

Settlement pattern studies indicate that the Proto-Elamites arrived at Tepe Yahya following a period of regional settlement collapse and increased nomadism. The Proto-Elamites inhabited Tepe Yahya, and probably other sites in eastern Iran, for less than a century, introducing a social technology of control which previously was unknown to the region: tablets, seals and sealings, standard measurements of volume (beveled-rim bowls), and units of length measurement (the Yahya Kuš: Beale 1978, 1983). The reason(s) for the abandonment of the proto-elamite "colonies" on the Iranian Plateau remain entirely elusive. Whether they were assimilated by local populations or returned to their homeland (Khuzistan ?) cannot at present be determined. Following the abandonment of settlement by the Proto-Elamites at Tepe Yahya there is a discontinuity of material culture suggestive of a chronological gap. Certain it is that at Tepe Yahya, Shahr-i Sokhta, Hissar (?), Malyan, and Sialk, there is no continuity in the use of texts, beveled-rim bowls, standardized units, sealings, and only the rare presence of cylinder seals. The administrative structure and social order, as represented by these earlier artifacts, is nowhere sustained; nevertheless, following the proto-elamite presence numerous regional urban centers emerge in the absence of this earlier administrative technology of control.

I consider several of the observations made by Peter Damerow and Robert Englund, in their study of the texts from Tepe Yahya, of exceptional importance. Foremost of these is their observation, confirming my long-held suspicion, that "The level of these administrative notations, the size of the recorded animals and humans and the measures of grain, are without exception entirely within the range of *local* activity" (authors' emphasis). The agricultural production at Tepe Yahya appears to have been undertaken by "slaves or low-rank workers" who obtained rations in return for their labor. The system of production appears to have been based upon servile labor obligations (forced deliveries and forced labor) in which the direct producers were tied to a tributary mode of production. The absence of texts dealing with the production of local resources, metals, stone vessels, etc. would seem to suggest that the community was not involved in petty commodity production (i.e., small-scale capitalists), while servile labor in return for rations as wages argues against the presence of free wage labor. While the authors' study is enormously helpful in identifying the semantical hierarchy in the format of the proto-elamite administrative documents and offers a clear exposition of the various numerical systems, particularly the ŠE system for counting measures of grain, we are left uninformed by the tablets as to whether at Yahya "they were only inspired by or were in direct contact with an external political center."

Indeed, the relationship of the proto-elamite administrators to the rest of the community remains virtually unknown, as does the relationship of the various classes of primary producers both within the proto-elamite community at Yahya and between it and related communities. What is observable, however, is the descriptive presence of a *remarkable* phenomenon which involved a vast area of the Near East - from eastern Iran to northern Syria, from Shahr-i Sokhta to Tell Gubba. The phenomenon over this broad area has its material evidence in the distribution of identical seal types (so-called glazed steatite) and seal styles: the piedmont style; beveled-rim bowls, together with other ceramic types. On the Iranian Plateau the above cultural inventory is found associated with proto-elamite tablets. The social conditions giving rise to this phenomenon as well as the specific social relations that characterized it remain poorly understood. The genesis of the phenomenon may be embedded in the earlier Uruk centralization of southern Mesopotamia and its spread northward to distant Hassek Höyük in southeastern Turkey and eastward to Godin Tepe and Susa in Iran (Lamberg-Karlovsky 1985).

The proto-elamite phenomenon results from the assimilation by the Proto-Elamites of the earlier Uruk social technology. The social experiment toward a tightly controlled and administered social order is, however, neither sustained by the Uruk culture nor its later protoelamite or North Syrian variants. In a few short centuries within Mesopotamia, North Syria, and the Iranian Plateau, the legacy of the Uruk and proto-elamite phenomena is realized in the abundant presence of regional urban centers controlling smaller communities in the neighboring countryside. Archaeological evidence is, however, virtually non-existent for the social context in which this process must have unfolded - the presence of conflict and warfare. We are still a very long way from understanding the processes involved. Perhaps, with the development of a wider ranging comparative historical sociology we shall be able to overcome the arbitrary division which encumbers us, one that separates a positivist 'causal' analysis from a historicist 'interpretive' understanding.

We are left to puzzle over just what the Proto-Elamites were doing at Tepe Yahya. Were they as I have argued elsewhere (Lamberg-Karlovsky 1986b) characterized by a "domestic mode of production," an entirely self-sufficient community unaligned to a larger political entity? Or were they part of a closely coordinated centralized state (or even conquest empire) directed by a "capital," i.e., Susa, Malyan, or some other center? Are we dealing with a commonality of material culture, something on the order of a horizon-style, which is indicative of a technology of social control, administration and bureaucracy which nevertheless has little to do with centralized state formation but indicates regional lineage formations? How does one explain the existence of a two-hectare site such as Tepe Yahya (with only one other Period IVC site located within a radius of 30 km) manifesting all attributes of urban administration that characterized Mesopotamian communities half a millennium later? Is Tepe Yahya a peripheral community of some unlocated regional urban political center (i.e., the later Marḫaši of Mesopotamian texts, see Steinkeller 1982)? Lastly, how can we formulate hypotheses that permit us to determine which of the above ideas among many others are "historically" correct?

In answer to some of the above questions I briefly summarize the hypothetical process reconstructed in more detail in the forthcoming report on the third millennium at Tepe Yahya. At Uruk (southern Mesopotamia: Middle Uruk period), and a century or two later as Susa (Khuzistan: proto-elamite, Jemdet Nasr period) both regions were settled by ethnically and linguistically distinct (Amiet 1979) communities of competing "peer-polity interaction" (Renfrew and Cherry 1985). The internal development of these competing communities, that is, *within* southern Mesopotamia and Khuzistan, were further characterized by their mutual competition with each other as distinctive 'states.' Within each of the peer-polities (Sumerian and proto-elamite) internal and external competition led to upward spiralling costs and downward marginal returns; that is, increasing costs accrued in maintaining an administrative bureaucracy, networks of communication, agricultural and commodity production, resource procurements, etc. As society evolves toward greater complexity, the costs to each individual within that society substantially increase; at a certain point, however, the costs may exceed the benefits derived. When this occurs economists refer to the "law of diminishing marginal utility" (Hailstones 1976). In ancient societies, dependent as they are entirely upon human, animal, and plant productivity, the solution to declining marginal returns can be accomplished by territorial expansion and the exploitation of new resources, land, people, etc.

This is precisely the phenomenon we see in the Uruk and proto-elamite expansion and "colonization" of regions distant from their "heartlands." Increasing management and production costs within the Sumerian and proto-elamite peer-polity interaction spheres led, in sequence, to the same response: the colonization of peripheral areas. This process led in turn to two immediate benefits: a reduction of population pressure within each (Sumerian and proto-elamite) peer-polity (Adams 1981; Johnson 1987) and an increase in new resources and productivity within the 'colonies.' The limits of territorial expansion, within pre-industrial societies, are dependent upon the expanding powers' ability to maintain their logistic of transport, communication systems, garrisoning costs, and expenditures for conquest. At a certain point the expanding power will confront an invisible frontier wherein costs for maintaining the colony or expanding beyond far exceed benefits. The investment in a policy of territorial expansion may initially greatly benefit the "heartland," resulting in a marginal return that is most favorable. This appears to be true for both the earlier Sumerian and proto-elamite "heartlands" as well as within their respective "colonies." In both instances, however, the Uruk and proto-elamite "colonies" within a century collapse. Why?

The collapse of the "colonies" signals within each area of their presence a decline in the level of socio-political complexity and the severing of ties to their regional polities (Sumerian and proto-elamite). The earlier articulated system of "heartland" and "colony" initially had a benefit/cost ratio which was extremely favorable in terms of economic productivity. Within a very few generations the initially high marginal return began to decline. The costs of administration, both within and between 'colonies,' logistics of transport, communication, and the presence of a potentially subversive local population (why else the walls around Habuba Kabira or Godin Tepe) made the costs inordinately high while the benefits were increasingly marginal. The upward-spiralling competitive costs and downward marginal returns saw a common, though most likely chronologically sequenced, response: collapse! Tainter (1988:198) has commented upon this process in a most lucid manner:

> "... under a situation of declining marginal returns collapse may be the most appropriate response. Such societies have not failed to adapt. In an economic sense they have adapted well - perhaps not as those who value civilizations would wish, but appropriately under the circumstances" (author's emphasis).

Communities, nations, and empires wax and wane for reasons that many authors attempts to adduce. In a little known but splendidly insightful essay, *Metallurgy as Human Experience*, the distinguished historian of metallurgy Professor Cyril Stanley Smith (1977:6) has written:

> "These and hundreds more materials and uses grew symbiotically through history, in a manner somewhat analogous to the S-curve of a phase transformation in the materials themselves... There was a stage, invisible except in retrospect, wherein fluctuations from the status-quo, involving only small localized distortion, began to interact and consolidate into a new structure; this nucleus then grew in a more or less constant environment at an increasing rate because of the increasing interfacial opportunity, until finally its growth was slowed and stopped by depletion of material necessary for growth, or by the growing counter-pressure of other aspects of the environment. Any change in conditions (thermo-dynamic = social) may provide an opportunity for a new phase. We all know how the superposition of many small sequential S-curves themselves tend to add up to the giant S-curve of that new and larger structure we call civilization... Because at any one time there are many overlapping competing sub-systems at different stages of maturity but each continually changing the environment of the others, it is often hard to see what is going on. Moreover, nucleation must in principle be invisible, for the germs of the future take their validity only from and in a larger system that has yet to exist. They are at first indistinguishable from mere foolish fluctuations destined to be erased. They begin in opposition to their environment, but on reaching maturity they form the new environment by the balance of their multiple interactions. This change of scale and interface with time, of radical misfit turning into conservative interlock, is the essence of history or anything whatever, material, intellectual or social."

C.C. Lamberg Karlovsky
Harvard University

Introduction Bibliography

Adams, R. McC.
  1981   *The Heartland of Cities*. Chicago: University of Chicago Press.

Amiet, P.
  1979   "Archaeological Discontinuity and Ethnic Duality in Elam." *Antiquity* 53:195-204.

Amiet, P. and M. Tosi
  1978   "Phase 10 at Shahr-i Sokhta Excavations in Square XDV and the Late Fourth Millennium Assemblage at Sistan." *East and West* 28:9-31.

Beale, T. W.
  1978   "Bevelled-rim Bowls and their Implications for Change and Economic Organization in the Late Fourth Millennium B.C." *Journal of Near Eastern Studies* 37:289-313.

Beale, T. W. and S. M. Carter
  1983   "On the Track of the Yahya Large Kuš: Evidence for Architectural Planning in the Period IVC Complex at Tepe Yahya." *Paléorient* 9:81-88.

Caldwell, J.
  1967   *Investigations at Tal-i Iblis*. Illinois State Museum, Preliminary Reports, No. 9, Springfield, Illinois.

Dyson, R. H., Jr.
  1987   "The Relative and Absolute Chronology of Hissar II and the Proto-Elamite Horizon of Northern Iran" in O. Aurenche, J. Evin, F. Hours, eds., *Chronologies in the Near East*. BAR International Series 379, Oxford.

Hailstones, T. J.
  1976   *Basic Economics*. Cincinnati: South-Western Publishing Co.

Johnson, G.
  1987   "The Changing Organization of Uruk Administration on the Susiana Plain" in Frank Hole, ed., *The Archaeology of Western Iran*. Washington: Smithsonian Institution Press.

Lamberg-Karlovsky, C. C.
  1971   "Proto-Elamite Account Tablets from Tepe Yahya, Southeastern Iran." *Kadmos* X:97-99.
  1971b   "The Proto-Elamite Settlement at Tepe Yahya." *Iran* IX:87-96.
  1976   "The Third Millennium of Tepe Yahya: A Preliminary Statement." *Proceedings of the IVth Annual Symposium on Archaeological Research in Iran*. Iranian Center for Archaeological Research, Teheran: 71-84.
  1985   "The *longue durée* of the Ancient Near East" in J. L. Huot, M. Yon, and Y. Calvet, eds., *De l'Indus aux Balkans*. Editions Recherches sur les Civilisations, Paris.

Lamberg-Karlovsky, C. C. and M. Tosi
  1973   "Shahr-i Sokhta and Tepe Yahya: Tracks on the Earliest History of the Iranian Plateau." *East and West* 23:21-57.

Reindell, I. and J. Riederer
  1978   "Infrarotspektralanalytische Untersuchungen von Farberden aus persischen Ausgrabungen." *Berliner Beiträge zur Archäometrie* 3:123-134.

Renfrew, C. and J. Cherry
  1985   *Peer Polity Interactions and Socio-Political Change*. Cambridge: Cambridge University Press.

Smith, C. S.
  1977   *Metallurgy as Human Experience*. American Society for Metals, Metals Park, Ohio.

Steinkeller, P.
  1982   "The Question of Marhaši: A Contribution to the Historical Geography of Iran in the Third Millennium B.C." *Zeitschrift für Assyriologie* 72:237-265.

Tainter, J. A.
  1988   *The Collapse of Complex Societies*. Cambridge: Cambridge University Press.

Catalogue of the Tepe Yahya Texts

Tablet	Room/Area	Provenience	Page in Manuscript
1	5	B.70.20-1	32
2	5	B.70.20.1	34
3	5	B.70.20.1	36
4	5	B.70.20.1	37
5	5	B.70.20.1	37
6	5	B.70.20.1	38
7	1b	BM.71.3.3	39
8	5	BM.71.4.8	51
9	1b	BM.71.3.3	40
10	1b	BM.71.3.3	41
11	1a	A.75.11.2b	53
12	C	A.75.11.3a	59
13	C	A.75.11.3a	58
14	1a	A.75.11.2a	41
15	1a	A.75.11.2b	43
16	C	A.75.17.11.3	43
17	1a	A.75.11.2a	44
18	1a	A.75.17.11.2	45
19	1a	A.75.17.11.2	46
20	1a	A.75.11.2b	47
21	1a	A.75.17.11.2b	48
22	C	A.75.17.11.3	49
23	C	A.75.11.3a	49
24	C	A.75.11.3a	50
25	B	A.75.11.7	50
26	C	A.75.11.3a	60

THE PROTO-ELAMITE TEXTCORPUS*

The archeological background

The publication in the 1920s and '30s of substantial collections of archaic texts from Mesopotamia was accompanied by a lively discussion of the position these early tablets held in the
development of the very widely attested cuneiform script. The archaic tablets from Uruk and
other Babylonian sites were not, however, the first archaic texts from Western Asia to appear
in publications of epigraphists and Near Eastern archeologists. More than twenty years earlier,
numbers of decidedly archaic texts were unearthed in a region east of southern Babylonia
known in cuneiform documents of the 3rd millennium B.C. as "Elam."[1] The first of these
"proto-elamite"[2] texts to appear, two in number, were discovered during J. de Morgan's excavations at the end of the 19th century in Susa, the urban center of the Susiana Plain of 4th
and 3rd millennium Persia. Since V. Scheil's cursory treatment of these texts in 1900,[3] some

---

*In this volume, we have used in addition to the usual abbreviations in Assyriological literature the following: *ATU* 1
= A. Falkenstein, *Archaische Texte aus Uruk* (Berlin 1936); *ATU* 2 = M. Green and H. Nissen, in cooperation with P.
Damerow and R. Englund, *Zeichenliste der Archaischen Texte aus Uruk* (Berlin 1987); *BBVO* = *Berliner Beiträge zum
Vorderen Orient*; *CahDAFI* = *Cahiers de la Délégation Archéologique Française en Iran* (Paris); *ERBM* = J. Friberg,
The Early Roots of Babylonian Mathematics I and II (Göteborg 1978-1979); *Scrittura* = P. Meriggi, *La scrittura
proto-elamica* I-III (Rome 1971-1974); TY = Tepe Yahya (in tablet identification numbers). A discussion of the complex stratigraphy of Susa and its relevance to the chronology of the period treated in the present paper has for the
most part been avoided; reference is made throughout to the levels determined in the acropolis excavations of 1969-
1971 (cf. A. Le Brun, "Recherches stratigraphiques à l'Acropole de Suse, 1969-1971," *CahDAFI* 1 [1971] 163-216).
"Susa 17" is thus an abbreviated reference to Susa Acropolis I 17. We wish to thank R. Dittmann, FU Berlin, for his
helpful comments on an earlier version of this paper, as well as B. André and M. Salvini for their permission to col-
late the *MDP* texts and to see the unpublished Susa texts housed in the Louvre, Paris.

[1]The geographical designation "Elam" was represented in Mesopotamian cuneiform texts with the sumerogram NIM,
which may in general be translated "high(land)"—this is what the region appears to be from the perspective of the
inhabitants of the Babylonian alluvial plain. The indigenous Elamite designation was Ḫa(l)tamti, for which W. Hinz,
CAH I/2³, 644, offered a possible etymology "god's land" from ḫal 'land' and tamt '(gracious) lord'; "Elam" may be an
akkadianized rendering of both Sumerian and Elamite terms influenced by *elûm*, "to be high."

[2]We have chosen the following terminology for the earliest stages of script development in the ancient Near East:
the terminus "proto-elamite" is a description of an historical phase in the Susiana plain and the Iranian highlands sit-
uated to the east of Mesopotamia. This phase is generally considered to correspond to the Jemdet Nasr/Uruk III and the
ED I periods in Mesopotamia, and is represented in Iran by the levels Susa 16-14B (including, possibly, part of 17A)
and corresponding levels from other sites (i.e. Yahya IVC, Sialk IV.2, Late Middle Banesh [Banesh Building Level
II], etc.). It may be dated to ca. 3050-2900 B.C. The same term is used to describe the earliest documents from the
region inscribed with both numerical and ideographic signs, which are assumed to represent in written form a geneti-
cally related precursor of the Old Elamite language attested ca. 2300 B.C. The evidence for this assumption seems
very meager (cf. fn. 14 below to P. Meriggi's attempts in this regard), so that "proto-elamite" as a qualification of
archaic tablets from Persia must, for the time being, be understood as a conventional term. Similar terminological
difficulties have arisen from the treatment of the earliest written documents from Mesopotamia. To avoid any direct
and, in our opinion, misleading links between the script of these tablets and the Sumerian language—links which
seem equally unfounded at present (cf. P. Damerow and R. Englund, *ATU* 2, 150²²; R. Englund, "Administrative
Timekeeping in Ancient Mesopotamia," *JESHO* 31 [1988] 131-133⁹)—we qualify archaic Mesopotamian texts with
the term "proto-cuneiform," thus precluding the necessity of referring to the language(s) which may have been represented by the early script. In this connection, all "Sumerian" readings of proto-cuneiform signs in the present paper
are to be understood as entirely conventional; they are, for the purposes of convenient reference, all taken from the
signlist *ATU* 2.

[3]*MDP* 2, 130-131. The first of the published tablets has been treated *in extenso* by J. Friberg, *ERBM* I, 22-26.

1,450 proto-elamite tablets from Susa have been published,[4] there remaining but few unpublished texts from that site in museums in Paris and, presumably, Teheran, as well as in some collections acquired through the antiquities market.[5] Recent excavations of other proto-elamite sites have proven that the script and numerical systems from Susa were in broad use, indeed covering an area greater than that of the more or less contemporaneous Uruk III writing system employed in Mesopotamia. Tablet finds from Tepe Sialk to the north, from Shahr-i Sokhta to the east,[6] from Tepe Yahya to the south and from Susa to the west[7] imply a geographical range of the proto-elamite script of ca. 300,000 square kilometers[8]. Attempts to explain the dramatic spread of proto-elamite culture and consequent script use into even very small settlements such as Tepe Yahya have been numerous. Some have considered the existence of tablet collections and related material goods found outside of Susa to be the result of a

---

[4]The following count of text copies (excluding photo publications) may serve as a preliminary reference: 208 tablets in *MDP* 6 (including with the publication numbers 399 and 4996 the two tablets edited in *MDP* 2), 490 in *MDP* 17, 649 in *MDP* 26 and 26S(upplement), and 50 in *MDP* 31. For a compact review of the *MDP* publications and of tablet findspots cf. W. Brice, "The Writing System of the Proto-Elamite Account Tablets of Susa," *Bulletin of the John Rylands Library* 45 (1962-1963) 17-20 and F. Vallat, "The Most Ancient Scripts of Iran: The Current Situation," *World Archaeology* 17 (1986) 335-347, esp. 338-339. Some 40 additional Susa tablets have been published in scattered articles (R. de Mecquenem, *RA* 50 [1956] 202; F. Vallat, *CahDAFI* 1 [1971] figs. 43 and 58; id., *CahDAFI* 3 [1973] 103; M. Stolper, *CahDAFI* 8 [1978] 94-96).

[5]Some 100 unedited proto-elamite fragments currently housed in the Louvre are being prepared for publication by M. Salvini. The small number of proto-elamite tablets which found their way into private collections via the illicit antiquities market or otherwise is a welcome contrast to the lamentable situation known from Mesopotamia. We are aware of no such proto-elamite collections with more that twenty tablets.

[6]It is not at present possible to definitively date the tablet from Shahr-i Sokhta (P. Amiet and M. Tosi, *East and West* 28 [1978] fig. 16), and those from Tepe Sialk (R. Girshman, *Fouilles de Sialk* I [1938] pl. 92-93). Tepe Sialk covered both of the phases late Uruk and proto-elamite, there being however very few finds there of tablets of the proto-elamite phase (the chronological difficulties represented by the Sialk levels IV.1 and IV.2 were first clarified in R. Dittmann's 1983 contribution "Susa in the Proto-Elamite Period ..." in U. Finkbeiner and W. Röllig, eds., *Ğamdat Naṣr: Period or Regional Style?* [Wiesbaden 1986] 184-186+86; cf. id., *Betrachtungen zur Frühzeit des Südwest-Iran* Teil 1 [=BBVO 4/1; Berlin 1986] 294-297, P. Amiet, "La période IV de Tépé Sialk reconsidérée" in J.-L. Huot et al., eds., *De l'Indus aux Balkans* [=Fs. Deshayes; Paris 1985] 293-312 and id., *L'âge des échanges inter-iraniens* [Paris 1986] 66-69, 110-112, and R. Dyson, op. cit., 660-664). Only S. 28 of Sialk IV.2, published by Girshman in *Fouilles* and in *RA* 31 (1934) 115-119, is clearly of the common proto-elamite script. F. Vallat, *CahDAFI* 1, 243, assigns this tablet according to ductus to Susa 16 and consequently the other tablets to Susa 17; cp. R. Dyson, op. cit., 663. The other tablets, all found in Sialk IV.1, are either rather clumsily drawn, lacking the classical proto-elamite linear format (see below), including S. 1626 and 1630 in *Fouilles* pl. 92 and S. 1620, 1623 and 1624 on pl. 93, or are "numerical tablets."

[7]The most important finds outside of Susa are the texts from Tal-e Malyan, for which see M. Stolper, *Kadmos* 24 (1985) 6-8, in part duplicated and expanded by the publications W. Sumner, *Iran* 14 (1976) 103-115 + pls. IIId, e and h, E. Carter and M. Stolper, *Elam: Surveys of Political History and Archaeology* (Berkeley 1984) 253 and I. Nicholas, *Expedition* 23/3 (1981) 45.

[8]This range may increase with the resumption of survey activity and excavations in Iran. Just one inscribed tablet has been unearthed at Tepe Hissar southeast of the Caspian Sea, with the findnumber H 76-122 (unpublished, courtesy of M. Tosi). The deposit layer with which the tablet was in association has given a calibrated radio-carbon date of 3650-3370 B.C. (cf. B. Hurst and B. Lawn, *Radiocarbon* 26/2 [1984] 222, P-2766; reference from M. Vidale and A. Lazzari). This dating, the associated material complex and the text ductus suggest that this tablet will likely prove not to be proto-elamite; see R. Dyson, "The Relative and Absolute Chronology of Hissar II and the Proto-Elamite Horizon of Northern Iran," in O. Aurenche et al., eds., *Chronologies du Proche Orient* (=BAR International Series 379; Oxford 1987) 647-678, esp. 659-660 to the "clay tag or label with three non-Proto-Elamite signs or symbols" and to the tablet blanks found in context possibly corresponding to Susa 17 or "17x" (Dyson's "proto-elamite transition"; cf. fn. 37 below). The Godin Tepe V "numerical tablets" (tablets with numerical, but lacking ideographic signs and, based on the Susa stratigraphy, generally dated to the late Uruk period) published by H. Weiss and T. Young, "The Merchants of Susa," *Iran* 13 (1975) 9-10, further, belong to a level corresponding to late Uruk/Susa 17 and are thus not to be classified as "proto-elamite." The same applies for the tablet from Choga Mish published by E. Porada, *Archaeology* 22 (1969) 58, number 432 A.

gradual cultural diffusion; in which local populations borrowed together with cultural elements the *idea* of writing from the developed Susiana tradition.[9] Others entertain the thesis that these tablets are evidence of colonial activity originating in the capital city, either in the

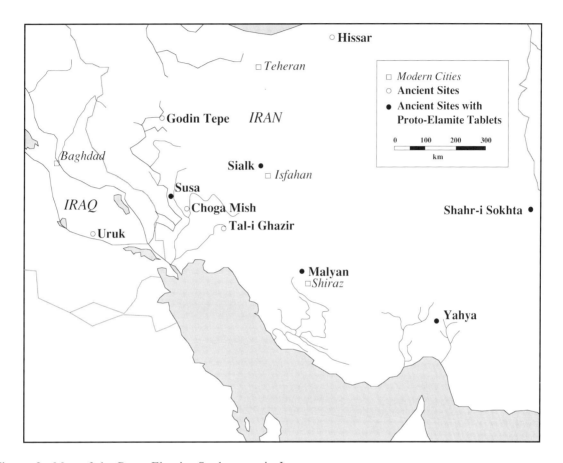

Figure 3. Map of the Proto-Elamite Settlements in Iran.

form of direct imposition of political will or in the form of traders' settlements along the lines of Kanesh in central Anatolia.[10] It appears on the basis of archeological evidence most probable that involved demographic developments, in particular population pressures, effected the movement and eventual settlement of population blocks across Iran.[11]

[9]Two very informative recent contributions to this discussion are C. Lamberg-Karlovsky, "The Proto-Elamites on the Iranian Plateau," *Antiquity* 52 (1978) 114-120 and J. Alden, "Trade and Politics in Proto-Elamite Iran," *Current Anthropology* 23/6 (December 1982) 613-640 (cf. fn. 171 below).

[10]Quite aside from the fact that the tablets found there deal explicitly with matters of exchange, Kanesh itself exhibits an archeological picture different from that of proto-elamite sites. Whereas the Kanesh trader colony is distinguishable from the indigenous Anatolian culture only through the presence of its archives, the Iranian tablet finds are without exception in context with other, so-called diagnostic material goods of the proto-elamite phase.

[11]For this suggestion, cf. for example the discussion of C. Lamberg-Karlovsky, "Further Tracks on the Earliest History of the Iranian Plateau," paper presented at the *Second USSR/USA Archaeological Exchange in the Archaeology of the Ancient Near East, Central Asia, and the Indus,* Samarkand, USSR, 8-22 September 1983 (published in part in the *Information Bulletin of the International Association for the Study of the Cultures of Central Asia* 6 [Moscow 1984] 49-53, as "The *longue durée* of the Ancient Near East," in J.-L. Huot et al., eds., *De l'Indus aux Balkans,* 55-72, and as "Third Millennium Structure and Process: From the Euphrates to the Indus and the Oxus to the Indian Ocean,"

Little more than the mere existence of documents from settlements scattered across the Iranian plain is usually offered as written evidence for such conjectures. Information culled from the texts themselves which might support or refute historical models has for the most part been entirely wanting. Despite the fact that these texts are not deciphered, the necessary preliminary work on the formal characteristics of the proto-elamite inscriptions, that is work on the categorization of ideographic and numerical notations into semantical and arithmetical groupings, has begun. We shall in the following attempt to describe the current state of decipherment and to present the results of our work on the texts from Susa and, specifically, from Tepe Yahya.

Previous work on the proto-elamite tablets

The French excavations of Susa and the extensive tablet finds made there have offered the basis for work in the past 90 years on the proto-elamite texts. The results of decipherment, both for linguistic and historical analysis, have, however, been disappointing. The practices of the early excavators have been widely criticized and require here no further comment than that tablet finds are consequently in an unlucky state of documentation. Indeed, only with the advent of the modern French field research were control excavations made which allowed of a serious stratigraphy and thus relative chronology of the heretofore published text corpus.[12] Critical *archival* relationships may, however, be irrevocably lost; only the very time-consuming work of building a complete textual data base—whether computerized or simply based on parsed transliterations—offers any hope of partially reconstructing the administrative archives which should tell us so much about the organization of proto-elamite society in Susa.

Interest in past work on poorly deciphered Western Asian scripts such as proto-elamite has centered, more than on the advance such a study promises in the delineation of the paleographical development of the studied script in particular and of writing in general, on an increase in the philological understanding of existing or of extinct but related languages underlying those scripts. In the case of proto-elamite, some effort has been expended trying to demonstrate a link between this and the presumably related Old Elamite script, which saw limited use during the Old Akkadian period.[13] Syllabic sign readings adduced from these studies have however led to no successful decipherings of the archaic script. A preliminary graphotactical analysis of the proto-elamite texts has also met with only modest success.[14]

OrAnt. 25 [1986] 189-219). Lamberg-Karlovsky operates here with the working hypothesis that proto-elamite culture spread as the result of the necessary dispersion in an economy characterized by a "domestic mode of production" (a primitive mode of production still in the hands of primary producers). This interpretation is based by and large on the assumed absence in the proto-elamite tablets found outside of Susa of shared personal titles and the attestation there of only small quantities of goods. The latter point seems a valid one; the former one remains however suspect until all personal titles in Susa texts are gathered and compared with those in texts from other sites. At least the signs we consider designations of "low status workers," ⊱ and ⪺ (see the discussion below of the texts TY 11-13), are common to Susa, Malyan and Yahya.

[12]Cf. A. Le Brun, *CahDAFI* 1, 163-216.

[13]Cf. W. Hinz, "Problems of Linear Elamite," *JRAS* 1975, 106-115; P. Meriggi, *Scrittura* I, 184-220.

[14]P. Meriggi, "Der Stand der Erforschung des Proto-elamischen," *JRAS* 1975, 105 and *Scrittura* I, 172-184, isolated 50 of the signs most commonly used in presumable personal names. Our preliminary analysis of the proto-elamite

Advances in proto-elamite studies have been hindered to a certain degree by the lack of necessary philological tools. A first step in such textual work leading to a complete edition of the proto-elamite texts would be the availability of a signlist sufficiently dependable and cleansed of redundant sign variants as to offer, first, a rough idea of the number and the frequency of use of signs in the scribal repertoire, and second, a transcriptional instrument capable of delivering for analysis sign combinations and simple contexts in a form understandable to the participating decipherers. The two early editors of the Susa texts, V. Scheil and R. de Mecquenem, opted for signlists which contain as many of the signforms as possible, thus achieving, in the case of the final signlist in *MDP* 31, a sign repertoire of some 5,500 signforms (including the signs from the Old Elamite inscriptions then known). While we know for example that logographic scripts can have large sign repertories at their disposal,[15] still of the 5,500 signs in *MDP* 31 so many are clearly redundant variants that a substantial reduction in the number of entries should be possible.[16] A chronological division of the texts may reduce, at least for specific periods, this signlist even further.

This was in fact the stated goal of P. Meriggi's signlist *La scrittura proto-elamica* I-III (Rome 1971-1974). *Scrittura* is however more than a compilation of proto-elamite signs; it represents the first attempt to offer a systematic analysis of the complete proto-elamite textcorpus. Volume I of the series ("La scrittura e il contenuto dei testi") contains a formal classification of the texts, a description of text format and a referenced analysis of certain classes of ideograms in the script, including those for "humans" (pp. 39-50), "animals" (pp. 50-66), "grain products" (pp. 66-78), etc.[17] This valuable contribution to the field of proto-elamite studies suffers, however, from a number of flaws, which in our opinion severely impair the usefulness at least of the signlist proper (Volume II) and, necessarily, of the text transliterations (Volume III). The large section in Volume I (pp. 159-172) devoted to "numbers" is, in the first place, replete with untenable interpretations; as a consequence of in particular

---

texts suggests that scribes writing such titles may have followed conventions of sign sequence stricter than those used in proto-cuneiform sources. There may thus be reason to believe that an evaluation of this graphic characteristic will eventually deliver critical information about the language underlying the proto-elamite script. The results of Meriggi's statistical analysis of these signs according to such standard criteria as frequency of initial or final position appear, however, to offer little encouragement. In the first place, the rather numerous exceptions to Meriggi's implied rule of standardized sign sequence noted by W. Brice in *Bulletin of the John Rylands Library* 45, 28-29 and esp. 32-33, put in doubt the reliability of any results of the analysis. Meriggi's assumptions that "Proto-elamite" was a precursor of Old Elamite and that personal names were written syllabically, moreover, are unsupported. Given the span of ca. 700 years unaccounted for between proto- and Old Elamite, and given the high probability of the use in proto-elamite personal names of logographic signs, some of which by means of phonetic transfer will likely have developed into syllabic signs by the Old Akkadian period, a determination of any genetic relationship between Old Elamite and the language possibly represented by the proto-elamite texts seems to us at present impossible. See I. Gelb, "Methods of Decipherment," *JRAS* 1975, 95-104, for a sobering view of the prospects for further decipherment, based on conventional cryptanalytical methods, of such scripts as the proto-elamite.

[15]The most often cited example of nearly complete logography, the Chinese script, contains between 40,000 and 50,000 signs. This number, achieved primarily through the construction of sign combinations, may however be some 100 times higher than the basic number of Chinese signs (recorded in the *Shuo-wen* lexicon of ca. 100 A.D.).

[16]Many redundant variants could be determined in the proto-cuneiform documents due to the Mesopotamian lexical tradition of writing and copying lists of words, adhering to the same sequence of signs over periods of up to 1000 years and longer. The exploitation of such lists was instrumental in the compilation of the new signlist of the archaic texts from Uruk, *ATU* 2. No such lucky circumstance is known from the proto-elamite corpus, so that redundancy in that script must be isolated exclusively on the basis of contextual sign usage.

[17]Our interpretations, which for the most part differ only in details from those of Meriggi, are presented in the commentaries to the Yahya texts below.

Meriggi's false interpretation of the numerical system used to represent grain quantities,[18] combined with his transcription of all numerical notations, disregarding their respective systems, into Roman numerals, the reliability of a large number of text transliterations is made doubtful. We are moreover not in agreement with Meriggi's often unsubstantiated and, as we believe, misleading Latin transliterations of certain key signs. The transliteration of the sign ⟨sign⟩ with JUGUM, for instance, is incompatible even with Meriggi's own interpretation "child" of the sign ⟨sign⟩,[19] which is often attested together with ⟨sign⟩; the resulting sign combination would have to be interpreted as "yoke-child" or the like. While the utility of the signlist proper may be questioned from a philological standpoint—many of his groupings of the *MDP* 31 signs into some 400 forms remain in any case open to question—the idea of a simplified grouping of graphically comparable signs is a good one, assuming it is founded on a vigorous contextual sign analysis. Taken together, the flaws of *Scrittura* would not of themselves have precluded the use of its signlist were it not for the existence of purely technical mistakes. In numerous cases, the sign forms cited by Meriggi were mirror images of the signs on the proto-elamite tablets and thus could not be referred to in publications without exhausting explanations and cross-references.[20]

A. Vaiman's important 1972 paper "A Comparative Study of the Proto-Elamite and Proto-Sumerian Scripts,"[21] while expanding on the description of the formal characteristics of the proto-elamite texts begun by W. Brice and P. Meriggi,[22] succeeded in establishing the clear direct connection between the proto-elamite and proto-cuneiform numbersigns and numerical systems—in contrast to the situation known from the ideographic signs. That there was little clear evidence for the borrowing of *ideograms* from the Mesopotamian into Persian writing systems or vice versa was already obvious to the first editors of the archaic texts, V. Scheil and S. Langdon. The few attempts made in this direction, in particular those of A. Falken-

---

[18]See our discussion below of the so-called ŠE system.

[19]The sign is, contrary to his own transliterational system, represented by Meriggi with the Sumerian word TUR, "small (human)," "child," which is on two counts a questionable interpretation. In the first place, the archaic "Sumerian" sign TUR is probably a pictographic representation of "breasts" (cf. *ŠL* II/2, 144; the sign is of uncertain application in the proto-cuneiform texts: at least small children of the category SAL+KUR/"GEME₂" [⟨sign⟩] seem to have been designated with the sign ŠA₃ [with or without a qualifying TUR; cf. *ATU* 2 s.v.] or, in Uruk IV documents, with the numerical sign ⟨sign⟩ also used to count juvenile cattle). In the second, the proto-elamite sign ⟨sign⟩ seems more likely to be a qualification of humans corresponding to proto-cuneiform KUR (⟨sign⟩; conventionally translated "male slave"). Cf. the commentary to TY 11 below.

[20]The sign ⟨sign⟩ is in Meriggi's list the simple mirror image ⟨sign⟩ (no. 56), ⟨sign⟩ is ⟨sign⟩ (no. 367c). Mirror images are on the whole easily corrected; in many cases, however, it is impossible to identify the exact sign meant in the signlist without consulting the original text copies. For example, ⟨sign⟩ is in the signlist ⟨sign⟩ or ⟨sign⟩ (nos. 346 and 346b), ⟨sign⟩ is ⟨sign⟩ or ⟨sign⟩ (in Meriggi's signlist, all sign forms are rotated 90° to the right relative to conventional depiction; cf. below, fn. 30).

[21]*VDI* 1972:3, 124-133 (in Russian with English summary p. 133; available to us in a German translation to appear in *BagM* 20 [1989]).

[22]W. Brice, *Bulletin of the John Rylands Library* 45, 15-39; id., "A Comparison of the Account Tablets of Susa in the Proto-Elamite Script with those of Hagia Triada in Linear A," *Kadmos* 2 (1963) 27-38; id., "The Structure of Linear A, with some Proto-Elamite and Proto-Indic Comparisons," in W. Brice, ed., *Europa: Studien zur Geschichte und Epigraphik der frühen Aegaeis* (=*Fs. E. Grumach*; Berlin 1967) 32-44; P. Meriggi, *Scrittura* 1; id., "Comparaison des systèmes idéographiques mino-mycénien et proto-élamique," in M. Ruipérez, ed., *Acta Mycenaea* 2 (=*Minos* 12, 1972) 9-17.

stein, S. Langdon and P. Meriggi, were, although ad hoc identifications, having been based exclusively on graphic similarity, at least suggestive of some contact between the two writing centers of the archaic period.[23]

The real dynamic represented by the numerical signs in the further decipherment of proto-elamite was documented in J. Friberg's *Early Roots of Babylonian Mathematics*, vol. I, published in 1978. Beyond clarifying the until then misunderstood structure of the archaic numerical system used for grain measures, Friberg demonstrated that the ever-present numerical notations in the archaic—proto-cuneiform as well as proto-elamite—documents were very powerful tools in the semantic identification of a number of ideograms, including those for grain products and those for animals and, it seems, humans.

Berlin work on archaic texts

Our work in Berlin has centered on the preparation for publication of the ca. 4800 for the most part fragmentary archaic tablets from Uruk. The Uruk Project, under the direction of H. Nissen and supported jointly by the Free University of Berlin and the Deutsche Forschungsgemeinschaft, has in recent years expanded into an intensive cooperation with P. Damerow's research group "Cultural Development and Cognition" at the Center for Development and Socialization of the Max Planck Institute for Human Development and Education, Berlin. This cooperation has resulted in an ongoing investigation of the development of conceptual thought in early civilizations, in particular our investigation of the early concept of number.

The growing emphasis in Berlin on the analysis of the numerical systems in the proto-cuneiform texts effected the broadening of the subject matter to include two important topics. First the preliterate material from the Near East, including the so-called "numerical tablets," the bullae both with and without sign impressions and the geometrically shaped pebbles, which have been the topic of intensive study by, in particular, D. Schmandt-Besserat.[24] Second the substantial archaic tablet collections discovered in Persia. Although there are striking differences of script and format between the proto-elamite and the proto-cuneiform tablets, the comparability of the numerical systems and, it seems, of a number of semantic categorizations in the two writing systems seemed to make imperative the inclusion of the proto-elamite texts in our further research on the archaic texts from Mesopotamia. We were encouraged in this

---

[23]P. Meriggi has summarized these identifications in "Altsumerische und proto-elamische Bilderschrift," *ZDMG* Spl. 1 (1969) 156-163, esp. p. 163, Abb. 5-6. The list of some 150 sign equivalencies compiled by R. de Mecquenem in *MDP* 31, p. 147 and pls. LXVIII-LXX, seems equally without semantic support. I. Gelb, *A Study of Writing* (London 1952) 217-220, has warned against attaching great importance to such graphic identifications, since many pictographic representations are likely to be similar even in disparate cultures. The possible derivation of the proto-elamite sign ✝ from the proto-cuneiform ⊕ (UDU, "small cattle"), both being obvious abstractions, is however suggestive of a real borrowing. Cf. to this sign the commentary below to TY 11.

[24]For her work, cf. fn. 61 below and the literature cited in the bibliography in this volume. A theoretical discussion of conceptual development leading to arithmetical thinking is found in P. Damerow, "Die Entstehung des arithmetischen Denkens" in P. Damerow and W. Lefèvre, eds., *Rechenstein, Experiment, Sprache* (Stuttgart 1981) 11-113 and id., "Individual Development and Historical Evolution of Arithmetical Thinking" in S. Strauss, ed., *Ontogeny, Phylogeny and Historical Development* (Norwood, New Jersey, 1988) 125-152.

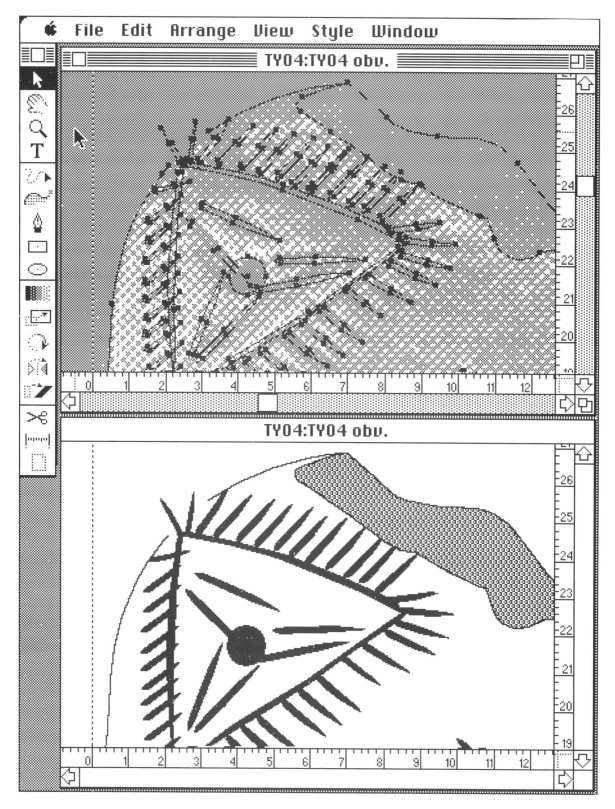

Figure 4.   Use of graphics in copying the Yahya texts. Above: drawing surface; below: simultaneously displayed window with results.

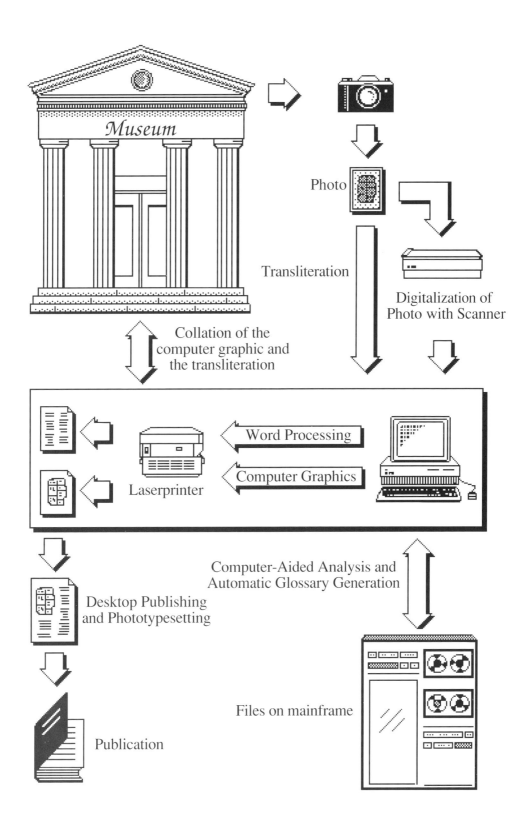

Figure 5. Standard procedure in the copying and editing of archaic tablets.

endeavor by the initial success of J. Friberg's examination of the proto-elamite texts from Susa, and presented our preliminary results in a working paper at the Third Berlin Colloquium on Concept Development in Babylonian Mathematics in December 1985.

Although we have discussed in a separate paper some of the techniques currently used by our project to deal with the imposing number of proto-cuneiform tablets now being prepared for publication,[25] it will be helpful to make some general statements about the consequences these methods should have for the process of analyzing and preparing for publication archaic texts and about their particular application in the case of editing the tablets from Tepe Yahya. Since a nearly complete data base of all proto-cuneiform texts has been established on a mainframe computer of the Free University, we have in our work on the decipherment and edition of archaic texts from Mesopotamia concentrated our efforts on the high promise presented by computer-assisted methods employing an artificial intelligence programming environment. As a consequence of our experience with computers having computational capacity insufficient for the application of AI methods on mass data, we have opted for the use of a Siemens Interlisp programming environment on a Siemens mainframe 7.580E. Siemens Interlisp is an implementation of Interlisp-D, which is a major Lisp dialect used primarily on Lisp workstations, but much more powerful when used on a high-speed mainframe. We use an expanded version of Interlisp 4.01 developed for our special purposes by a Siemens program development group headed by D. Kolb in Munich.

Despite the close relation between proto-cuneiform and proto-elamite texts, the latter texts have not yet been included in our data bank due to the difficulties of transliteration resulting from the lack of a dependable signlist. The Yahya texts treated here were however stored by using the signlist compiled by R. de Mecquenem in *MDP* 31. Methods developed for our work on the very much larger Uruk corpus could thus be used to compile sign indices of the Yahya texts.

We are presently supplementing these methods of electronic data processing with applications of computer graphics. One practical application of the new possibilities afforded by dramatically improved graphics and layout programs on personal computers is their use as a complement to traditional handcopying methods in producing and printing tablet copies. Such an application seems to us particularly suited to the needs of copying the very curvilinear and plastic, yet uncomplicated signs common to archaic texts, and we have begun this work with some success on the Uruk III period texts from Jemdet Nasr. All copies appearing at the end of the present paper were produced with standard graphics software specific to the Apple Macintosh system we presently employ. Photographs of the Tepe Yahya texts were first digitalized with a flatbed scanner and read into the computer's software to act as templates below empty drawing surfaces for first drawings (see Figure 4). These preliminary copies are normally taken into the museum housing the original tablets to be corrected by hand. The results of this work are then themselves rescanned to serve as templates for the final copies,[26] which

---

[25]P. Damerow, R. Englund and H. Nissen, "Zur rechnergestützten Bearbeitung der archaischen Texte aus Mesopotamien," *MDOG* 121 (1989; in print).

[26]In the case of the Yahya tablets in Teheran, no collation of our copies was possible. We believe, however, that the control afforded us by the existence of field textcopies (cf. our remarks below) is sufficient to justify publication of the copies in their present form.

can be printed directly using a common laser printer (300-400 dpi) or, as in the present case, in offset quality (1200 dpi) on a phototypesetting machine. An overview of these procedures is offered in Figure 5. All graphics embedded in the present text were also realized on the same computers. These methods offered a solution to the problem of finding an understandable format for the publication of the Yahya texts in that we were able to choose, in a fashion suited to our needs, the method common in earlier treatments of undeciphered scripts of a conventionalized graphic reproduction of the texts.[27] This is in our opinion a good compromise between the demands of printing and the necessity of a transliteration which does not overtax a reader's industriousness. We are also examining the possibility of building up a graphical data bank of all the proto-elamite texts. At present, the excessive demands of graphics on limited storage capacity have made serious work in this direction impossible.

The current paper has resulted from the friendly suggestion of D. Potts, at the time a faculty member of the Department of Near Eastern Archeology of the Free University of Berlin, that we study, in conjunction with our work on the archaic texts from Mesopotamia and Susa, the texts excavated at Tepe Yahya, and from the request of the director of the Yahya excavations, C. Lamberg-Karlovsky, that we prepare a written analysis of the Yahya texts to complement his final excavation reports.[28] To both of them we wish here to extend our gratitude for the opportunity to work on this small but very informative text archive.

TEXT STRUCTURE

Format of the texts

Not only the material of the proto-elamite texts, namely clay, but also their general shape correspond to usage in Babylonia. The clay was as a rule formed into rather thick, oblong tablets,[29] which seem normally to share the relation of length to width of ca. 3:2 common to Babylonian tablets.[30]

---

[27]Cf. for one example P. Meriggi, *Acta Mycenaea* 2, 9-17.

[28]A preliminary analysis of the Yahya texts prepared by P. Meriggi was made available to us by Lamberg-Karlovsky; we are grateful to have been able to use this manuscript, which we are however unable, for understandable technical reasons, to cite. For the direction of the paper, cf. Meriggi's initial treatment of the texts TY 1-6 in *Scrittura* I, 220 and III, 148 and 176.

[29]S. Langdon, *Pictographic Inscriptions from Jemdet Nasr* (=*OECT* 7; Oxford 1928) p. VIII, mentioned as well the observation of V. Scheil that convex faces of the proto-elamite tablets were invariably the obverse sides, as is common in Mesopotamian practice.

[30]We continue here to follow in the direction of script and thus tablet "length" and "width" the convention of Assyriologists; like the Mesopotamian tablets of the 4th and 3rd millennium B.C.—cf. the persuasive evidence offered by F. Picchioni, "La direzione della scrittura cuneiforme e gli archivi di Tell Mardikh Ebla," *Or.* 49 (1980) 225-251 (information repeated in German and English in *Sumer* 42 [1979-1981; appeared 1986?] 48-54 and *Studi Orientali e Linguistici* 2 [1984-1985] 11-26 respectively)—the proto-elamite tablets were written and read from a perspective turned 90° to the right of their depiction in the present and, for instance, in the early *MDP* publications. This conclusion is not only supported by the pictographic depiction of animals, in particular equines, with heads in an upright position (cf. for example the text *MDP* 17, 105). The use of Babylonian numerical signs is also instructive: they are impressed in the same position relative to these pictograms as we would expect them in Mesopotamia. The few examples of proto-elamite ideographic signs engraved in cylinder seals, moreover, show these signs, like their counterparts in Mesopotamia, in a position relative to pictorial depictions on the seal such that the conventional

As was already convention in Mesopotamia of the earliest proto-cuneiform phase, Uruk IV, the proto-elamite scribes utilized both sides of a clay tablet. Generally speaking, the reverse seems, as in Uruk, to have been reserved for a summation of multiple numerical entries on the obverse. Irrespective of the space remaining after two or more entries on the obverse, the scribe invariably, if any summation was made, rotated the tablet around a horizontal axis and inscribed the total of the entries along the left edge of the reverse. There are however exceptions to this rule. Summations may appear in different positions on the reverse

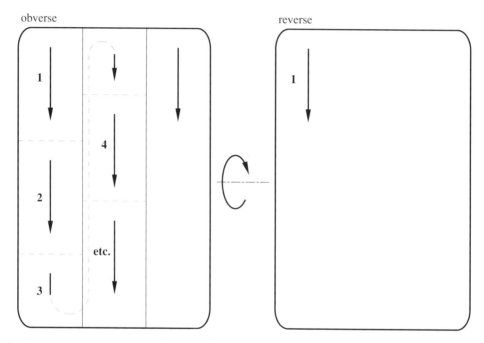

Figure 6. Proto-elamite tablet organization. The numbers 1, 2, 3, ... indicate the heading (1) and individual text entries (2, 3, 4, etc.).

of tablets.[31] The axis of rotation, moreover, seems as in Mesopotamia not to have been a scribal convention of overriding importance.

When more space for separate entries was required than available on the obverse of a

perspective of tablets would have to be turned 90° to the right (compare in particular the sign ⯈ // ⯈ often used as a global text heading in proto-elamite texts from Yahya, Susa and Malyan [see below] with the sign ⛛ in the sealings collected by L. Legrain in *MDP* 16 [1921] pl. 17, nos. 266 and 268, pl. 23, no. 330, with the sign ⛛ on pl. 3, no. 53 [cp. the same on a sherd from Yahya IVC (A 11-5) in D. Potts' contribution in C. Lamberg-Karlovsky and D. Potts, *Excavations at Tepe Yahya: The Third Millennium* (forthcoming)] and with ⛛ on the the the seal P. Amiet, *MDP* 43/2, 1108; the sign ⊠ attested in TY 13 and often in the Susa corpus may correspond to a sign ⛛ on the seal published in 1900 by V. Scheil, *MDP* 2, 129). It may be underscored in this connection that nearly all abstract ideograms and numerical signs in the proto-cuneiform and proto-elamite sign repertories, given that the tablets were written turned 90° to the right of conventional publications, were drawn symmetrically relative to a vertical axis imagined through the middle of the sign. Thus the conventional depictions of the proto-cuneiform signs AB, "(Persian) gulf" (?): ⯇, BA, "eye": ⊖, GADA, "flax(-drying apparatus ?)": ⪦ must be rotated 90° to be symmetrical relative to a vertical axis: ⟁, ⯑ and ⋀. The Yahya signs ⊠, ⊰ and ⥈ also exhibit the same symmetry only when turned 90°: ⊠, ⛛ and ⛛.

[31]*MDP* 17, 45, for example, contains a total written in the middle of its reverse.

tablet, the scribe continued these entries on the reverse. After rotating the tablet around the horizontal axis, however, he began inscribing the reverse from the upper left corner, where normally the total would have been written. This procedure was contrary to the practice in Mesopotamia of continuing along the right edge of the reverse and working to the left, which usage was an important part of the bookkeeping system, always leaving the left edge free for totals and summary information about tablet contents, including date formulae.[32] Once the tablets were stacked together in shelves or baskets, this part of accounts remained available for quick inspection. The often only fortuitous adherence to this rule in the proto-elamite texts can be understood as an indication that those tablets were not similarly stored.

Entries on the obverse of a tablet often commenced in the upper left corner with a general heading, followed by one or more individual entries. These were inscribed in lines from top to bottom kept in columns defined, if at all, by having simply pressed the shank of the stylus along the length of the tablet. No apparent organizing importance was attached to the end of these columns; the notation of a particular entry often began in a column at the bottom of a tablet, and continued at the top of the adjoining column. This phenomenon is particularly obvious in the many examples of numerical notations spread across two such "columns." It seems the scribe only recognized the separating relevance of the columns when he inscribed a notation in the cereal numbersign system $\check{S}^{\#}$ (see our discussion of this phenomenon below). Custom dictated that this entire notation be encased in a rectangle of etched strokes; if he recognized that a complete notation in $\check{S}^{\#}$ could not be accommodated in the remaining space at the bottom of a column, the scribe left that space free and inscribed the notation in the next column.[33]

The tablets from Tepe Yahya exhibit an entirely parallel format. In all four obvious cases in which numerical notations of individual entries were subsumed in totals, TY 1, 2, 7 and 18, the individual entries are to be found on the obverse, the summations in the left-hand column of the reverse. With the exception of TY 1, all were furthermore rotated on a horizontal axis.[34] All entries and column ordering of the Yahya texts, finally, follow the same linear sequence noted for the Susa texts.

Semantical hierarchy

According to our analysis, the proto-elamite administrative texts may be divided into three major sections. Many texts begin with a sign or a sign combination which qualifies all transactions recorded in the text and which never contains a numerical notation. Such a sign or sign combination is termed here a *heading*. The actual content of the texts consists of one or more individual sub-sections which exhibit a clearly recognizable, standardized structure. As the

---

[32]A. Vaiman, *VDI* 1972:3, 130-132, has remarked that texts without summations were rotated around a (in our terminology) vertical, texts with summations around a horizontal axis. A similar idea was expressed by W. Brice, *Bulletin of the John Rylands Library* 45, 20-21.

[33]See the discussion below to TY 5 and 21.

[34]The possible function of the use of the vertical axis in the rotation of TY 1 remains unclear to us. TY 8 and 19, although with no obvious totals, were rotated on a horizontal axis.

result of their clear formal structure, we are able to isolate and identify these distinct text units as individual text *entries*. We find in the proto-elamite corpus multiple-entry documents which exhibit different levels of internal entry organization. Texts may consist simply of a linear se

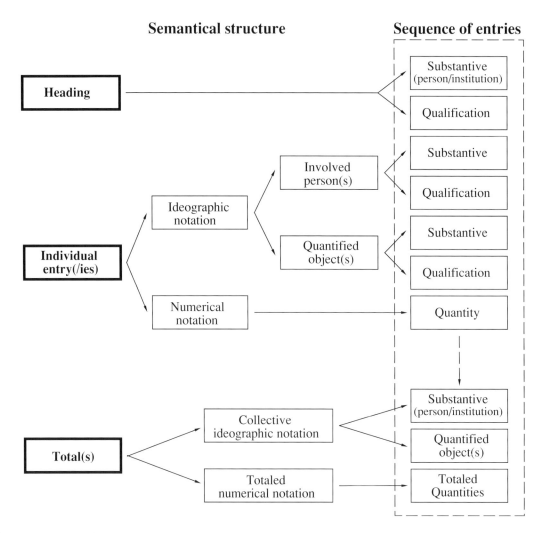

Figure 7. Hierarchical structure of the proto-elamite administrative documents.

quence of entries of exactly the same type. An example of such a text structure would be a list of grain rations for a number of different recipients. Texts may reflect in their entries a hierarchical order of transmitted information. A simple example is the often encountered alternation of two different types of entries such as a number of workers followed by the amount of grain allotted them. In this case, the two entries may be considered as being consolidated in a higher text unit. Texts may however be highly structured with many identifiable levels of hierarchy, reflecting for instance the organizational structure of a labor unit.[35] Particular entries of a higher order which we call *totals* contain summations of numerical notations from all or some entries together with collective ideographic notations. The general structure of the proto-

---

[35]A good example is the text *MDP* 6, 4997 analyzed in fn. 153 below.

elamite texts is such that they always consist of one or more entries and may or may not contain an initial heading and one or more totals or sub-totals. It is worthy of note that all entries seem to contain a numerical notation. They therefore seem to represent more the structure of a system of bookkeeping than the division of a spoken language into distinct sentences or other comparable semantic units.

The semantical structure discussed here proves the close relationship of the proto-elamite to the proto-cuneiform corpus. Proto-elamite headings correspond to general subscripts often accompanying totals of proto-cuneiform texts. Entries in proto-elamite documents correspond to "cases" of proto-cuneiform texts; while the hierarchical structure of individual proto-elamite entries is already on the whole a semantical structure no longer reflected in the syntactical structure of linear entry sequence, in proto-cuneiform texts this hierarchy is in some measure still represented directly by the graphical arrangement of cases and sub-cases.[36] Although represented in graphically different forms, proto-elamite texts thus exhibit the same general semantical structure as that of proto-cuneiform texts. This relationship between the semantical and the syntactical structure of the proto-elamite and proto-cuneiform texts must be considered a strong indication of their relative chronology. If we are to assume that a transfer of the idea of writing took place in 4th millennium Western Asia, then the more developed separation of semantics and syntax evident in the proto-elamite texts would testify to the antecedence of the proto-cuneiform corpus. This view would be in full accord with the established stratigraphical correspondences between Susa and Uruk. Archeological evidence from Susa imposes a synchronism between the early levels of Uruk III (the second Babylonian writing phase) and Susa 16 and possibly 17"Ax", in which the first proto-elamite tablets were unearthed or should be dated.[37]

Not only the structure, but also the relative complexity of the Tepe Yahya texts discussed in the present paper are in full accord with the complexity and structure of the proto-elamite texts from Susa. Of the 18 Yahya texts whose beginning is preserved, 11 have an initial heading,[38] the others seem to begin with the first entry.[39] Most of the texts contain multiple entries in a simple linear order, up to a maximum of 17 entries in the text TY 11; at least five texts seem to have only one entry, in one case without a heading.[40] Five texts allow of an identification of a hierarchical structure: the four texts TY 1, 2, 7 and 18 contain summations which are in the nature of compilations of products probably dispersed to different individuals, the text TY 12

---

[36]The graphic structure of the proto-cuneiform texts from Uruk was discussed by A. Falkenstein in *ATU* 1, pp. 5-12; cf. now M. Green, "The Construction and Implementation of the Cuneiform Writing System," *Visible Language* 15 (1981) 345-372.

[37]R. Dittmann, *BBVO* 4/1, 296-297 and 458, tab. 159e, discussed the presumed transitional period designated by him, following A. Le Brun, 17Ax or 17X. The "contact 16-17" proposed by Le Brun, *CahDAFI* 1, 210, is derived from unstratified material from earlier de Mecquenem excavations; tablets edited by F. Vallat, *CahDAFI* 1, 237 as "contact 17A-16" were apparently equally unstratified (cf. R. Dittmann, in U. Finkbeiner and W. Röllig, eds., *Ǧamdat Naṣr: Period or Regional Style?*, 171[1]). See also D. Schmandt-Besserat, "Tokens at Susa," *OrAnt.* 25 (1986) 93-125 + pls. IV-X; F. Vallat and A. Le Brun, *CahDAFI* 8, 11-59; R. Dyson, *BAR International Series* 379, 648-649.

[38]TY 1, 3, 4, 7, 9, 12, 14, 16, 19, 22 and 23.

[39]TY 2, 5, 11, 15, 17, 20 and 25.

[40]TY 4, 15, 16, 26 and 27, TY 15 without heading; we are unable, based on the photos at our disposal, to determine in all cases whether the unphotographed reverse sides of the texts cited were in fact uninscribed or perhaps destroyed.

contains a combination of two mutually dependent entries into a more involved unit of administrative information.[41]

Just as in Susa, special signs appear in the Tepe Yahya texts which seem preferably used in initial headings or, in seldom cases, as sub-headings of sections of larger accounts.[42] It is a striking fact that the same signs are employed as headings in the Susa as well as in the Yahya texts. Such signs usually do not act as ideographic signs in individual text entries. The best known of these headings, the "hairy triangle" ▷, is instructive in its characteristic use to qualify probable accounts. The sign serves in Susa as well as in Tepe Yahya—in 10 of 11 preserved headings—to form with various inscribed signs, especially the quadrilobe (✦) in Susa and Tepe Yahya, the trilobe (❧) in Tepe Yahya alone, a large number of composita. No known attestation suggests to us the use of this sign as an element either in personal names or in titles of individuals; rather, the frequent position of the sign as the first ideogram on the proto-elamite tablets indicates that it functioned as an introductory and global qualification of the body in whose name a particular transaction is recorded. The attestations of this and other signs employed as headings on contemporaneous cylinder seals is entirely consonant with its interpretation as the symbol of an institution, since *personal* seals, that is seals with an indication of personal ownership, are neither attested in seal inscriptions nor are they to be anticipated based on the late Uruk and proto-elamite designs which have been, to date, gathered and analyzed.[43]

Entries as a rule consist of a combination of, first, an ideographic and, following it, a numerical notation, occasionally followed by an additional ideographic element.[44] We reserve to a following section of the present paper a discussion of numerical notations. The ideographic notation assumes the initial position of an individual entry and seems almost exclusively to represent involved persons or quantified objects or both; when both appear in a given notation, sign combinations which we believe designate involved persons invariably precede quantified objects. Designations of persons consist of signs or sign combinations representing persons or titles, often introduced by a sign which represents the position the named person assumed in the organization. Object designations as a rule consist of an ideographic sign, often together with a sign or sign combination qualifying the object. We have as yet no statistical means to test the probability of certain signs having functioned as qualifications of presumed substantives.

A secure identification of the semantical category to which a particular sign or sign combination belongs is facilitated by the availability of a sufficiently large group of related texts. Nevertheless, even for the large Susa corpus, such identifications are often rife with

---

[41]The exact structure of the seemingly complex tablet TY 19 is unclear to us; cp. our remarks to this text below.

[42]Cf. the treatment of the proto-elamite text headings by W. Brice and P. Meriggi in the articles cited in fn. 22.

[43]Cf. R. Dittmann, "Seals, Sealings and Tablets," in U. Finkbeiner and W. Röllig, eds., *Ǧamdat Naṣr: Period or Regional Style?*, 332-366. C. Lamberg-Karlovsky, *OrAnt.* 25, 210 (s. fn. 11), has suggested that ▷ "represents the maximal group, i.e. the tribal confederation [in his "domestic mode of production"]; the sign which is placed within the triangle, which often stands as a sign alone, is representative of a smaller kin grouping, i.e. a tribe or lineage."

[44]This phenomenon is most obvious in the case of totals or following a final text entry; see for instance the final signs in the texts *MDP* 6, 213, 220, 358, 377 and *MDP* 17, 32.

difficulties, particularly in isolating ideographic qualifications from ideographic designations of persons and objects. A particular complication arises from the fact that the scribe could omit part or all of the ideographic element of any given entry when he deemed the element sufficiently obvious in the context of the text. Much greater are such difficulties in the case of the small text collection from Tepe Yahya, which offers few contextual sign occurrences for internal comparisons. Many of the object designations contained in the Yahya texts could be identified as such only by their comparison with corresponding signs from the Susa corpus. It is thus possible to identify as clear object designations the following Yahya signs: ⬦, ➢, ⤙, ▷, ◀, ⬭ and ▤. It is puzzling that although the sign best attested in the Yahya corpus as designating a cereal product, namely ≋, can be identified in the Susa texts, it seems not to have been used there in the same function. Furthermore, in the case of the sign combination ≋ ⤙ attested in TY 1, 5 and 19, it remains unclear which of the two signs is an object designation and which has a qualifying function. Similar difficulties may be registered for the sign ⬦. While it seems clearly to designate a cereal product in TY 1, it can also, for instance in TY 11, be part of a personal designation. We know of no clear attestation of this sign used to represent a cereal product in the Susa corpus, where it seems to appear *only* in personal designations. Numerous signs are either not or only doubtfully identifiable with counterparts in the Susa signary, for example the two signs ▨ and ᙁ, so that in texts like TY 14 and 17 we are unable to identify even the semantical categories of the entries concerned. In such cases we may expect some assistance only from a comparative analysis of all occurrences of formally parallel sign usages in the textcorpus.

We are fortunate to have in the Yahya texts TY 1, 2, 7 and 18 four clear totals. These totals exhibit no obvious differences to those in the texts from Susa. Formally, they are inscribed in the same fashion as an individual entry and consist of an ideographic and a numerical notation. Totals are, in comparison with individual entries, substantially more important for the information their numerical notations offer about the makeup of the numerical systems in use on the one hand, and for the opportunity their ideographic notations present to establish the semantic categories of the objects registered in the individual entries of the texts on the other. The ideographic notation of the total contains, optionally, the person or institution under whose responsibility the transaction recorded in the text took place, and a *general classification* of the objects involved. It is thus possible, based on such semantic classifications, to compile a variety of signs into a single semantic category. For instance, in Tepe Yahya the sign combination ≋ ⤙ is a generalized designation of objects represented by the signs ≋, ≋ ▨, ⬦ and ≋ ᙁ. Unfortunately, the Yahya texts which contain totals are all in a state of preservation which substantially reduces their value in this regard. Either the totals themselves or the individual entries of the texts are damaged, making necessary restorations which are, based on the photos at our disposal, not always convincing; explicit reference to such tenuous interpretations is made below. The ideographic combinations in the Yahya totals, moreover, cannot in all cases be plausibly explained. We shall have the opportunity to discuss these difficulties and the importance of semantic generalizations in the commentaries to the Yahya texts below, and refer here only to the interpretations of the signs ⬨ in TY 8 and ⟁ and ⬦ in TY 11.

NUMERICAL SIGN SYSTEMS

Early work on the numerical systems

V. Scheil offered as early as 1905[45] a preliminary analysis of the numeration used in the proto-elamite texts. The French scholar attempted in this initial work to subsume a large number of what we now know to be incompatible numerical notations from the proto-elamite texts at his disposal into one "decimal" system, including fractions of the basic unit "1" (▷) based on the later Sumerian sexagesimal usage of "1/6."[46] Scheil corrected this value in 1923[47] with his recognition of the fact that the next lower unit below "1," ⌒, represents not "1/6" but rather "1/5"; he however did not correct his assumption that all proto-elamite numbersigns belonged to a single numerical system.[48] His projection into the archaic period of a modern abstract conception of number, and thus of a unified numerical sign system, is understandable in an age which had yet little experience with a comparative ethnology of early arithmetical technologies.[49]

Scheil made a second contribution to the analysis of the proto-elamite numerical notations in 1935[50] with his short treatment of the notations used to record measures of grain ("ŠE system") and in particular with his preliminary edition of the text *MDP* 26, 362. This text, which is the only clearly recognizable school text in the proto-elamite corpus,[51] contains the summation of a number of cereal notations covering the entire range of possible notations of proto-elamite grain measures. It is thus of critical importance for the understanding of the correct relationships as well as the correct sign sequence in cereal notations, although some damage of the tablet surface combined with a probable scribal error to make a satisfactory reconstruction difficult.[52] Scheil allowed in his publication of the text for the advances in the understanding of the numerical notations used in archaic texts from Mesopotamia, and abandoned

---

[45]"Essai de déchiffrement des textes proto-élamites: système de numération proto-élamite," *MDP* 6, pp. 115-118.

[46]A diagram of Scheil's first attempt to make sense of the Susa numbersigns would take the following form:

[47]*MDP* 17, p. 3 to no. 17.

[48]Scheil determined further op.cit. pp. 6-7 to no. 45 the value of "100" for the sign ⌐⌐, which, as may be confirmed from his remarks pp. 28-29 to no. 443, he considered a variant of ●. Cp. S. Langdon's review of *MDP* 17 in *JRAS* 1925, 169-173.

[49]Scheil's incognizance of the development of numerical conception must be considered the first step in an extended history of a defective decipherment of a decimally structured numbersign system used in connection with measures of grain, which had very unfortunate repercussions in subsequent analyses not only of the grain measures system of the proto-elamite corpus, but also of the proto-cuneiform corpus, both of which in even very recent publications are still often referred to as "decimal" systems. Cf. *ATU* 2, 137g with fn. 46.

[50]*MDP* 26, I-VI.

[51]*MDP* 26, 362 appears, next to the proto-cuneiform text A. Falkenstein, *OLZ* 40 (1937) 402-406 and 409-410, no. 6 (cf. J. Friberg, *ERBM* II, 33-43), to be the second certain metrological "school text" in the archaic corpora; texts like *MDP* 17, 328 may be simple "exercises."

[52]The summations of the values above ▷ remain problematic in the text; a full treatment is impossible without a collation of the original in Teheran, which we suspect carries some erasures at least in the total on the reverse (we wish to thank J. Friberg for his comments to this text conveyed to us in a personal communication).

his abstract decimal system advanced in 1905. His identification of the values of the number-signs below "1" was correct, and he distinguished between numbers of discrete objects and notations of grain measures. He still assumed erroneously, however, that the sign ● had the same decimal numerical value of 10 times ▷ (instead of 6 times ▷) when representing grain measures as when representing numbers of discrete objects.[53]

This error is related to his correct observation of the strong links between cuneiform and proto-elamite numerical notations. The dependence both on the Babylonian numeration and metrology known from later tradition, as well as on the ensuing treatments of the archaic numerical systems made by F. Thureau-Dangin[54] and, following him, S. Langdon,[55] is however evident in Scheil's interpretation published in 1935 that the proto-elamite grain system was decimally structured and based on the sign ▷, which Scheil like Langdon[56] equated with a "gur" of 5 ◡ ="pi" (Sumerian barig), each "pi" of 60 "qa" (Sumerian sila).[57]

A much more solid foundation for work on the relations between proto-cuneiform and proto-elamite numerical systems was provided by a study of the Soviet scholar A. Vaiman. In 1972 he published an important paper with a formal description of the format of the proto-elamite texts together with an involved, although insufficiently documented, comparison of the proto-elamite with the proto-cuneiform numerical systems.[58] In particular, the nearly equal structure of the ŠE systems in the proto-cuneiform and proto-elamite documents was underscored by Vaiman, although he persisted in ascribing to both an erroneous decimal structure. In the same work he suggested that the use in the proto-elamite decimal system of one new sign and the new use of an old sign to express "100" and "1,000" (the signs ◁▷ and ⧖ respectively) should be understood as an indication of the borrowing of the writing system by the proto-elamite scribes from an established Mesopotamia tradition.

---

[53]This led to the assumption that lacunae in an original tablet, of which *MDP* 26, 362 was supposed to be a copy, were responsible for discrepancies in the summations: "Le total que nous obtenons, en opérant sur les données: 597.516 *gur* 40 *qa,* - paraît être inférieur de 15.606 *gur* 65 *qa* - au total officiel marqué au revers de la tablette: 613.122 *gur* 105 *qa"* (*MDP* 26, p. III). Instructive is also the difficulty with the text *MDP* 17, 153 expressed by both V. Scheil, *MDP* 17, pp. 21 and 26, and W. Brice, *Bulletin of the John Rylands Library* 45, 26 and 39, fig. 6. The simple addition in the text of 6 times 2 ▷ adding up to 12 ▷ = 2 ● (collated) was considered by both to be a scribal error rather than an indication that in grain measures ● might equal 6 ▷. Brice's strict adherence to the defective assumption ● = 10 ▷ in grain notations led him in his analysis of *MDP* 6, 4997 in op.cit. 31 to represent as a photo collation the emendation of a clear notation 1 ● 5 ▷ in the first entry of the text's second section into 2 ● 2 ▷ (thus with Brice 2 ● 2▷ + 1 ● 5 ▷ + 4 ▷ = 4 ● 1 ▷ instead of correctly 1 ● 5 ▷ + 1 ● 5 ▷ + 4 ▷ = 4 ● '2 ▷').

[54]F. Thureau-Dangin, "Tablettes à signes picturaux," *RA* 24 (1927) 29; id., "Notes assyriologiques LX: Le système décimal chez les anciens Sumériens," *RA* 29 (1932) 22-23.

[55]S. Langdon, *OECT* 7, pp. V and 63-68.

[56]Cf. *OECT* 7, pp. V and 64-66 to his "gur System."

[57]This final equation has no basis in the then known numbersigns; Scheil equated the smallest assumed member of the ŠE-system, ✦, equal to 1/12 —, to five qa and considered the sign ⬟ (see our discussion below of the ŠE system, esp. fns. 84 and 86) not a numbersign but rather an ideogram: "... signe littéraire ⬟ termine chaque compte particulier: il figure probablement un tas de grains, ou encore la couverture en coupole des greniers (*MDP* 26, p. III)." R. de Mecquenem, in his reanalysis of *MDP* 26, 362 in *MDP* 31 (1949) 40-42, demonstrated this interpretation to have been false; the sign ⬟ is rather the smallest attested member of the ŠE-system, representing a measure of grain 1/120 the size of ▷. He was thus the first to correctly identify all the numerical signs representing grain measures below ▷. In his analysis of *MDP* 26, 362, Mecquenem's values for the signs above ▷ remained, however, defective, therewith further cementing the fallacious theory of a decimal substratum of archaic numeration and metrology.

[58]*VDI* 1972:3, 124-133.

Doubtless the most important recent advance in the understanding of the proto-elamite numerical systems was made by the Swedish mathematician J. Friberg, whose work in the 1970s on, in particular, the Uruk III period texts from Jemdet Nasr published by S. Langdon in *Oxford Editions of Cuneiform Texts* volume 7, led him to study also the roughly contemporaneous proto-elamite texts from Susa. Friberg published in 1978 the preliminary results of his work in *ERBM* I, with a cursory representation of the proto-elamite numerical sign systems. In that work and in *ERBM* II (1979) he established for the first time that the ascription of a decimal structure to the archaic ŠE-system, initially made by Scheil in 1905, was incorrect; rather, this grain measurement system, as Friberg proved, exhibited a rather peculiar structure between the signs ⊏▷ and ◗, the most interesting element of which was the relationship ● = 6 ⊏▷[59] always overseen in previous work.

A new element in the study of proto-elamite numeration and metrology is the recent identification of a possible proto-arithmetical precursor of inscribed numerical symbols. The continuous use in Susa (and elsewhere) of a set of symbols to express probable numerical relationships from the pre- into the proto-literate period is a thesis discussed first by P. Amiet[60] and represented in recent literature most forcefully by D. Schmandt-Besserat.[61] The best documented treatment of this apparent precursor to the proto-elamite systems is an article published in 1978 by A. Le Brun and F. Vallat.[62] The authors presented clear evidence of the use in Susa 18 of sealed clay bullae to encase varying numbers of differently sized and shaped clay pebbles, which, following convention introduced by Schmandt-Besserat, are generally called "tokens." The impressions on the outside of the published bullae corresponded to the size and number of the enclosed tokens, insofar as these were accessible to examination, so that they could be used to correctly identify a correspondence between two tokens and the signs ● and ⊏▷ in documents from levels 17 and 16-14 ("numerical" and proto-elamite tablets respectively).[63]

---

[59]See our diagram below of this and two derived ŠE-systems in the proto-elamite corpus.

[60]*Elam* (Auvers-sur-Oise 1966) 70-71; id., "Il y a 5000 ans les Elamites inventaient l'écriture," *Archéologia* 12 (September/October 1966) 20-22.

[61]See the literature cited in the bibliography at the end of this volume, as well as that cited by Schmandt-Besserat, "The Origins of Writing," *Written Communication* 3/1 (January 1986) 45 and our comments in *ATU* 2, 148-149[12]. A complete and summarizing documentation of the available data is in preparation by Schmandt-Besserat.

[62]"L'origine de l'écriture à Suse," *CahDAFI* 8, 11-59.

[63]It remains for us a source of bafflement that the Susa excavator and epigraphist, like archeologists of other sites which have produced comparable bullae, have not split all bullae suspected of containing tokens. Such an action, which need scarcely be destructive of seals, would in the case of the unopened bullae S.ACR.I.77 2130.2 and 2162.1 (cited by Le Brun and Vallat in *CahDAFI* 8, p. 16) probably secure the identification of a further member of this set of preliterate numerical symbols including ● and ⊏, namely the circular impression (of a fingertip, according to op.cit., p. 15[5]) corresponding, against the common interpretation, to the sign — in the later ŠE-system, thus representing a measure of grain *less* than ⊏. This interpretation is offered by the sign's position relative to the sign ⊏ in all occurrences on bullae and tablets presented in *CahDAFI* 8 and on the bulla Sb 1940 in P. Amiet, *MDP* 43/1, p. 92, no. 555 (cf. id., *L'âge*, 83, no. 3 with fig. 31, p. 250), with the exception of the numerical tablet S.ACR.I.77 2128.2 (*CahDAFI* 8, p. 19 and 47, fig. 4, no. 2). Other alleged identifications of signs with higher values and of so-called "fractions" are for the most part based on mere speculation, finding little support in the primary sources. The values given in *CahDAFI* 8, p. 32, and by Vallat, *World Archaeology* 17 (1986) 337, mirror, moreover, fallacious assumptions concerning the numerical sign systems used in the later proto-elamite period. The critical review of such identifications recently published by Amiet in *L'âge*, 81-87, underscored the need to exercise caution in generalizing from few examples.

Comparison of proto-elamite with proto-cuneiform numerical systems

The first attempts to establish a clear relationship between the proto-elamite and proto-cuneiform scripts were concentrated on the conformity between the numbersigns and numerical systems used in the respective scripts. This conformity is already suggested by the fact that, contrary to the ideograms, the proto-elamite and the proto-cuneiform numerical signs exhibit the same sign forms. More importantly, the sequence of the basic signs (i.e., the combinations of vertical and oblique impressions of a round stylus) in the proto-elamite numerical notations corresponds to that of the proto-cuneiform notations, thus indicating that the scribes of the proto-elamite texts used numerical systems with at the very least the same quantitative order as known from the proto-cuneiform texts. This implies that the proto-elamite numerical signs exhibit the same arithmetical ambiguity as the proto-cuneiform numerical signs,[64] in that the numerical value of a particular sign differs according to its specific context of application. The exact quantitative relationships between the various members of an assumed system exhibited by the proto-elamite textcorpus could be inferred in many cases only by this analogy. But insofar as these relationships could be examined according to summations in the texts, they stood in exact conformity with the relationships of the proto-cuneiform numerical systems.

One difference between proto-cuneiform and proto-elamite numerical systems, however, has already been noted in earlier treatments. In addition to the sexagesimal and the bisexagesimal systems well known from the proto-cuneiform administrative texts as numerical systems used to count discrete objects, a strictly decimal system was used in certain areas of application. This numerical system finds, with two possible exceptions,[65] no parallel in the proto-cuneiform corpus.

An important result of our analysis of the proto-cuneiform numerical systems was the determination of ideograms which indicate in the texts the objects of the bookkeeping activities; this resulted in the confirmation that the numerical systems had distinctive areas of application. A comparably systematic analysis of the areas of application of proto-elamite numerical systems has not yet been undertaken due in large part to the difficulty in identifying the semantical function of the signs. The main reason for this difficulty is, of course, the inter-

---

[64]Cf. *ATU* 2, 117-121; 148-149[12].

[65]Both texts W7204,d (unpubl.) and W24189 (A. Cavigneaux, *UVB* 33-34 [forthcoming]) contain notations with multiples of the sign ⌐ ¬, whose only demonstrated archaic numerical use is in the proto-elamite decimal system with a value of "100." The latter, Uruk III period text exhibits the notations 7 ⌐¬ and ⌐3 ⌐ ¬ 1 ▷¬ in a context suggestive of an inventory of precious or semi-precious stones (an adjacent case has the sign NUNUZ/ZA₇; cf. *ATU* 2 s.v.). We suspect in this case that ⌐ ¬ represents an unknown quantity in an as yet undetermined numerical system. W7204,d contains as well a notation in damaged context with ⌐4 ⌐¬ [ ]; the presumably Uruk IV period tablet may however bear a stronger connection to Susiana, since it is sealed with a "wild boar" motif (W7204,b in *UVB* 5, pl. 25 [s. pp. 46-47] is doubtless a part of W7204,d; cf. also loc.cit., W6760,f/9850), which is also known from sealings unearthed in proto-elamite Susa (s. *MDP* 43/1, p. 97, nos. 599-600 with literature and cp. E. Strommenger, *Habuba Kabira: Eine Stadt vor 5000 Jahren* [Mainz 1980] 62, pl. 55, and *Ancient Near Eastern Texts from the Erlenmeyer Collection*, Christie's auction catalogue, 13 December 1988, p. 71, no. 21 [tablet now in the possession of the Metropolitan Museum, New York]). The two texts W20649 (unpublished) and 22115,9 (photo *ATU* 2, pl. 60, lower left corner) with the atypical notations [ ] ⌐1 ⌐¬2 ▷ 2 ● and 1 ⌐¬ 1 |● respectively are on the other hand at present only on formal graphical grounds to be compared to the proto-elamite sign ⌐ ¬, since they may attest to one or more as yet unknown numerical systems in the proto-cuneiform texts (see our comments in *ATU* 2, 147).

ruption of the paleographic tradition in Elamite sources: later Elamite texts, with the exception of the few Old Elamite linear texts, were written with Babylonian cuneiform. The most successful method in the semantic decipherment of proto-cuneiform signs, namely the establishment of paleographic continuity between archaic and later periods, is thus not applicable in proto-elamite research.[66] Most of the proto-elamite ideograms, moreover, are of a substantially more abstracted form than proto-cuneiform ideograms, whose pictographic character is often helpful in semantic analysis; the semantic analysis of proto-elamite is on the other hand largely dependent on the examination of contextual sign usages. It seems on the other hand that proto-elamite texts show the same close connection between numerical systems and the nature of the objects quantified by respective numerical notations. This connection may well help in future research to establish correspondences between proto-elamite and proto-cuneiform ideograms.

A discussion of the texts from Tepe Yahya will be served by a cursory introduction to the numerical systems evidenced by the proto-elamite texts from Susa, followed by a short discussion of the Susa systems which have been either confirmed or at the least reasonably postulated for the texts from Yahya. We have summarized in *ATU* 2, 117-166, the findings of our analysis of the systems used in the texts from Mesopotamia of the archaic periods Uruk IV-III, and have below made explicit the differences between the proto-elamite and the proto-cuneiform systems. The differences between the numerical systems attested in Susa and Tepe Yahya, also discussed below, are as might be expected of an entirely graphic nature and bear no evidence of semantical differentiation. It will be of interest to note in advance, however, that the unassuming graphical differences between the systems employed in Susa and Yahya to record measures of grain are not in evidence in the published and unpublished tablets from Malyan, which are in exact uniformity with texts from Susa.

Overview of proto-elamite numerical sign systems

The sexagesimal system S

The *sexagesimal* system used in Mesopotamia for most discrete objects, including domestic and wild animals and humans, tools, products of wood and stone and containers of in some cases standard measures, is also well attested in the Susa administrative texts,[67] although with

---

[66]Cf. above, fn. 14, to the on the whole fruitless attempts to establish semantic and even phonetic links between the proto-elamite and the Linear Elamite script.

[67]Among other objects qualified with numerical notations in the sexagesimal system are ●—• (*MDP* 6, 213 and *MDP* 26, 317), ═ with inscribed signs (*MDP* 26, 210), ◁ (*MDP* 17, 413 and *MDP* 26, 102-103), ◸ (*MDP* 6, 390 and *MDP* 26, 71), ◁◁ (*MDP* 17, 453 and *CahDAFI* 3, 103, no. 1) and possibly ◇ (cf. *MDP* 26, 314 and 461). Instead of the sign ▽, its inversum ◁ is used in *MDP* 17, 117, 413 and *MDP* 26, 108, 110 and 317. The only indication of the use in the sexagesimal system of ▽ to represent a quantity not, as usual, equal to but less than 1/2 ▷, is the notation

an obviously very restricted field of application.[68] The derived system S', whose function in archaic Mesopotamian documents we could not, despite the large number of references available to us, satisfactorily explain,[69] seems not to have been used in proto-elamite texts.

The bisexagesimal systems B and B#

According to our analysis of the proto-cuneiform texts, a second numerical system used to count discrete objects, the *bisexagesimal* system, registered primarily objects which seem to have been rations: for the most part barley products, but also among uncertain objects a special kind of fish and, possibly, cakes of cheese. Not only is in the proto-elamite texts the use of the same system apparent, but its application, as far as barley products are concerned, is also entirely parallel.[70]

The derived system B* of proto-cuneiform documents is not attested in the proto-elamite texts, but rather a graphically distinguished system B#.[71] Unlike the proto-cuneiform derived systems, the system B# is formed not by altering the individual sign, but rather by framing an entire notation. Such frames consist for the most part of discontinuous striations etched rectangularly around the complete notation; on occasion, this frame is rather carelessly drawn,[72] giving the impression of a notation akin to the proto-cuneiform system used to register quantities of grain of a particular type, the ŠE system Š*.[73] Judging from their relative areas of application, the two systems are not identical. Notations in the proto-cuneiform systems B and B* are, for instance, never added together; notations in the proto-elamite systems B and B# representing grain products can, on the other hand, be subsumed in a common total.[74] The graphic similarity to the proto-elamite ŠE system Š# (see below) as well as the parallel usage suggests that the system B# was used to register grain products containing amounts of grain recorded in the ŠE system Š#. A comparable relation between numerical systems is unknown in proto-cuneiform documents.

[ ]   1 ⊢ 5 ⌐ in *MDP* 17, 453. A similar ambiguity is attested in the proto-cuneiform system (cp. the use of ⌐ in the decimal system discussed below, and see *ATU* 2, 127 and 129).

[68]Semantic applications of the Mesopotamian sexagesimal system are shared in proto-elamite texts by the sexagesimal and the decimal systems; see the discussion below.

[69]Cf. *ATU* 2, 130-131.

[70]Cf. *MDP* 17, 421; *MDP* 26, 27, 50, 169, 349, 360, 386 and 467.

[71]Cf. *MDP* 26, 27, 50, 159, 162 and 360.

[72]Cf. *MDP* 26, 372, possibly also 441.

[73]Cf. *ATU* 2, 140-141.

[74]*MDP* 26, 27.

The decimal system D

```
            ⟨1000⟩
 "10000"  ←10 or:  ←10  "100"  ←10  "10"  ←10  "1"
            "1000"
```

A third system used to count discrete objects in proto-elamite texts which has no proto-cuneiform counterpart is the *decimal* system.[75] The area of application of this numerical system is usually interpreted as the registering of animals, including humans.[76] The correctness of this interpretation would imply that in the proto-elamite texts the area of application of this system corresponded to a part of the area of application of the proto-cuneiform sexagesimal system. That is to say, the proto-cuneiform sexagesimal system was used to register all discrete objects with the exception of rations. The proto-elamite sexagesimal system may have been used to count inanimate, the decimal system to count animate objects.

The ŠE systems Š, Š^# and Š″

The numerical system used to count measures of grain, the *ŠE* system (following conven-

---

[75]Cf. the texts *MDP* 6, 317, 399; *MDP* 17, 19, 45, 86, 105 and 275-277; *MDP* 26, 84, 156, 160-161, 171, 205, 217, 220 and 229. *MDP* 31, 31 (collated) and an unpublished fragment in the Louvre collection (M. Salvini, forthcoming) are the only witnesses known to us for the use of the variant graphs which combine the signs ⊠ and ⊠ with a sign resembling proto-cuneiform "GAL" (graphic form collated; the signform for "10,000" in the published text copy is incorrect), which may have been used as a semantic or phonetic determinative to avoid possible confusion of the decimal with the bisexagesimal system. The assumption that signs with the addition of "GAL" are only graphic variants of the basic forms is supported by the summation in this text:

$$2 \boxed{=} \; 5 \vdash \; + 1 \boxed{=} \; 2 \boxed{=} \; 1 \vdash \; + 1 \boxed{=} \; + 2 \boxed{=} \; 7 \vdash \; + 2 \boxed{=} \; 6^? \vdash \; + 2 \boxed{=} \; 7 \vdash \; = 2 \boxed{=} \; 3 \boxed{=} \; 6 \vdash.$$

[76]Texts discussed below in the commentaries to TY 11 and 12 seem to support an identification of the decimally counted objects represented by ⊥ and related signs with proto-cuneiform counterparts UDU, UDUNITA, etc. (small cattle; cf. *ATU* 2, 129) on the one hand, those represented by ⊃ and ⊂ with proto-cuneiform counterparts SAL and KUR (⊳ and ⊲; cf. *ATU* 2 s.v. and p. 129 with the literature cited in fn. 23) on the other; the use of the notations 2 ⌐ and 4 ⌐ in *MDP* 17, 184 to qualify presumable juvenile workers/slaves (assuming ⁚ is a variant of ⊡) is, moreover, similar to the use of ⌐ in Uruk IV period proto-cuneiform sources to represent, probably, the children of "slaves," there in parallel to the same use of ⌐ to denote young animals (cf. A. Vaiman, "The Designation of Male and Female Slaves in the Proto-Sumerian Script" [in Russian], *VDI* 1974:2, 138-148, esp. 142; article to appear in German translation in *BagM* 20 [1989]). If this interpretation is correct, the sign ⌐ should be considered a context-dependent variant of the normal unit ⊳.

tional usage with Sumerian ŠE = "barley," "grain"), employs signs of the sexagesimal system, however with entirely different arithmetical values. This system is as well attested in the proto-elamite as in the proto-cuneiform sources, and seems to have the same area of application. In particular, the small units (below ⬭) are, in the same manner as in Mesopotamia, used as qualifying ideograms for grain products, thus denoting the quantity of grain in one unit of the product.[77]

The proto-elamite ŠE system Š differs from the proto-cuneiform systems in the following manner: below ⬭ only units are used which are multiples of each other, thus simplifying the somewhat cumbersome use of the fractions employed in the proto-cuneiform texts (i.e., ⬭ = 1/3 ⬭ [this is the standard proto-cuneiform signform], ⬭ = 1/4 ⬭, etc.). A similar simplification may be found in the Uruk III period texts from the site of Jemdet Nasr, in which it seems scribes preferred to round small quantities in calculations and to use only the signs ⬭, ⬭ and ⬭ (1/3, 1/4 and 1/6 ⬭). The proto-elamite system Š, however, was more consequently linearized by continuing down to 1/12 and 1/24 ⬭; all relations between fractions of ⬭ were whole numbers. On the other hand, 1/4 ⬭, which in Jemdet Nasr was represented by a discrete sign, could and was often represented in proto-elamite documents by combining 1/6 and 1/12 ⬭, i.e., by the sign combination ⬭ ⬭. 1/3 ⬭, which was normally avoided in Jemdet Nasr by rounding, was represented in proto-elamite by a combination of 2 ⬭, which often assumed the form of a sign ligatur ⬭.

As is the case with the archaic texts from Babylonia, there seem to be numerical systems attested in the proto-elamite texts which were graphically derived from the basic system ŠE and which might have been applied to different sorts of grain. There is however no clear correspondence between the derived proto-elamite and proto-cuneiform systems. Best attested is the system ŠE#,[78] which seems related to the bisexagesimal system B#.[79] As in the case of the system B#, the striations framing a complete ŠE# notation are often carelessly drawn.[80]

A further derived system shares graphic similarity with the proto-cuneiform system ŠE", since the individual signs in a notation are impressed with two or more additional bars.[81] Whether all the signs with varying numbers of additional bars belong to the same system cannot, according to available documentation, be ascertained; the reverse side of the text *MDP* 17, 419, with a discrete notation including signs with both two and three additional bars, suggests that the number of bars employed with a notation in the proto-elamite system Š" was optional.

We have in *ATU* 2 presented the on the whole meager data allowing for an educated guess about the absolute sizes of the grain measures represented by the various members of the

---

[77]The use of these small grain units as part of sign composita representing grain products is much more common in proto-elamite than in proto-cuneiform texts (cf. for instance the texts *MDP* 17, 77, *MDP* 26, 349, 386, 467, *MDP* 26S, 4765 and the discussion of further similar texts in the commentary to TY 8 below). This phenomenon seems related to the use of NINDA$_2$ together with grain units in the proto-cuneiform texts, for which cf. *ATU* 2, 138.

[78]Cf. *MDP* 17, 2, 104, 228, 244; *MDP* 26, 357, 359; *MDP* 26S, 4785, 4841, 5223; *MDP* 31, 7.

[79]Cp. for example the texts *MDP* 26, 50 (system B#) with *MDP* 26, 359 (ŠE#). The text *MDP* 17, 104, moreover, contains notations in B# and ŠE#.

[80]Cf. *MDP* 26, 170, 402, 441 and 462 as well as the Yahya texts TY 1, 3, 7, 20 and 21 discussed below.

[81]Cf. *MDP* 17, 5, 9, 76, 149, 205, 213, 219, 243, 419; *MDP* 26, 44, 82, 95, 260; *MDP* 26S, 4804.

proto-cuneiform ŠE system. The basic underpinning of that analysis was the sign ⫞ (later Sumerian "ninda"), which is a clearly pictographic rendering of the beveled-rim bowl characteristic of all late Uruk period assemblages. This bowl in Uruk held, according to measurements made by H. Nissen,[82] between 0.6 and 0.8 liters of grain and could so be compared with the sila of later Sumerian tradition with between 5/6 and 1 liter volume. Further, we were able to document, citing primarily sources from Jemdet Nasr, that the sign ⫞ with few exceptions corresponded to the numerical sign 𒑰 or 1/6 of the grain measure represented by ⌣. This relation between ⫞ and 𒑰 is in our opinion entirely confirmed by the evidence presented in an article by one of us on Uruk period time notations, in which rations for a month of 30 days were represented by the sign 1 ▷ (= 30 𒑰).[83]

The occurrence of both beveled-rim bowls and of very nearly the same numerical systems for grain measures in archaic Persia as in Mesopotamia could indicate that the various numerical signs of the respective ŠE systems represented the same absolute volumes. At least two points recommend here however a cautious evaluation. In the first place, the proto-elamite ŠE system includes the sign ⏢ in the lower range less than 1/2 as large as the smallest arithmetically determined member of the proto-cuneiform system, ✸.[84] Assuming a mean value of 0.6 liters for the beveled-rim bowls in Susa,[85] we would have for the smallest measure a correspondence to the unusually small quantity of 0.15 liter.[86] In the second, texts discussed

---

[82]Cf. Nissen, "Grabungen in den Quadraten K/L XII in Uruk-Warka," *BagM* 5 (1970) 136-142 and G. Johnson, *Local Exchange and Early State Development in Southwestern Iran* (=Anthropological Papers of the Museum of Anthropology, University of Michigan, no. 51; Ann Arbor 1973) 129-139.

[83]Cf. R. Englund, *JESHO* 31, 121-185, in particular his treatment pp. 162-164 of the text *ATU* 1, no. 653. This relationship makes in our opinion untenable subsequent rebuttals of Nissen's thesis offered in particular by T. Beale, "Bevelled Rim Bowls and their Implications for Change and Economic Organization in the Later Fourth Millennium B.C.," *JNES* 37 (1978) 289-313 (offering bowls) and, most recently, by A. Millard, "The Bevelled-Rim Bowls: Their Purpose and Significance," *Iraq* 50 (1988) 48-57 (bread moulds).

[84]We have published in *MDOG* 121 a copy of an Uruk III period proto-cuneiform tablet from the recently auctioned Erlenmeyer collection which demonstrates that this sign listed in *ATU* 2 as N_{30c} represents not 1/6 but rather 1/10 of the quantity of grain represented by the sign N_{39}. The proto-elamite signform ⏢ used in our diagram of the ŠE system Š is based on our collation of the sign in the two reference texts *MDP* 6, 388 and *MDP* 26S, 4790. The proto-cuneiform signs N_{31} - N_{33} with up to 11 half-ovals around a central round impression (see the list of numerical signs in *ATU* 2) may have had some correspondence to the small proto-elamite units ✸ and ⏢; the signs are however attested in only one Uruk IV period text (*ATU* 1, no. 345) which offers no indication of the relative sizes of these signs.

[85]Cf. T. Beale, *JNES* 37, 289-313, with a range of ca. 0.4 - 0.9 l for archaic Persia. Beale presents pp. 300-303 data pertinent to the bowls from Yahya implying an intolerably large range of bowl sizes there. We are however not disconcerted by the volume variations in his figs. 9-11, since first a range in volume may be argued for various working categories–for instance, instead of only 10 or 15 sila per month as in Ur III Mesopotamia, the proto-elamite administration may have simply disbursed smaller rations daily to working children–and second a sample of 14 bowls is statistically insignificant. It should also be underscored that the bowls found would not have been measuring devices: these would have been only in the hands of disbursing agents, and exceedingly few in number.

[86]The sign ⏢ denoted a certain ration (?; cf. for example ⏢ in *MDP* 26, 324) and the amount of grain necessary for the production of a particular jar of beer; cf. the texts *MDP* 6, 388, *MDP* 26, 235 and 311 with the correspondence of the sign ⟁ to the numerical sign ⏢ (these three texts were treated by J. Friberg in *ERBM* I, 27-34; we reconstruct the first text with ◁• = 2 ✸ [cp. *MDP* 26, 340], ⊟ = 1 ✸ [collated; with presumably ⊰ = 1/2 ◁•] and according to collation a final entry ✸ 2 ⊳ [final numerical notation on right edge of tablet, not copied in *MDP*]). Even allowing for a weak beer, this would presume a jar size of less than 1 liter; we therefore suspect that spouted jars like those in L. Le Breton, *Iraq* 19 (1957) 99 fig. 13:6, A. Le Brun, *CahDAFI* 9 (1978) 111 fig. 24:9-10 and 149 pl. XIX:4 (Susa), W. Sumner, *Iran* 12, 163 fig. 5h[sic!] (Malyan) and R. Girshman, *Fouilles de Sialk* I, pl. 26, nos. 1-3 and pl. 88

below[87] show that the signs ⌇⌇ and ⌇⌇ which we interpret to represent worker categories were set in equivalence to 1/2 ⌇⌇ of grain. Assuming these texts deal with the regular monthly rations for these workers, 1/2 ⌇⌇ would have to stand in approximate correspondence to a one month ration for a worker in contemporaneous Mesopotamia, i.e., to 1 ⌇⌇. Although the possibility may therefore be entertained that the proto-elamite grain numerical signs represented measures roughly twice as large as those in Mesopotamia,[88] the testimony is by no means definitive[89] and we shall in the following text commentaries operate with the working hypothesis that the absolute values of the proto-elamite grain measures approximated those proposed for the measures in contemporaneous Mesopotamian sources.

The GAN$_2$ system G

The last numerical system we are able to isolate in the proto-elamite corpus is a system used to register surface measures and is called the *GAN$_2$* system G based on the common usage of this system in proto-cuneiform documents together with the sign GAN$_2$ representing an irrigated field. Only one proto-elamite text with a notation which may have been written in the system G, namely *MDP* 26S, 5224, can be cited. The text with the notation 1 ⬤ 8 ● 2 ⌇⌇ ⌐3 ⌇⌇⌐, although unique, should be considered a strong reference, since the signs 2 ⌇⌇ (2 "EŠE$_3$") are according to collation clear and not, as might have otherwise been suspected, a poor rendering of 4 ⌇⌇ and thus part of a ŠE notation. The diagrammed GAN$_2$ system assumes that the sign representing "10 BUR$_3$" ("BUR'U") in the proto-elamite corpus, ⬤, replaced the normal sign ◉[90] of proto-cuneiform documents; this is not an implausible assumption, since the same phenomenon is known from the archaic texts from Ur.[91] The possibility cannot however be excluded that the sign ● in MDP 26S, 5224, actually represented the corresponding sign "ŠAR$_2$" of proto-cuneiform texts, i.e., not 10 but 60 "BUR$_3$."

The similarity of the numerical systems next to major differences in the ideographic script brings us back to the relation between the proto-elamite and the proto-cuneiform script discussed above. It raises the question of whether the proto-elamite numerical signs were borrowed from the proto-cuneiform script or vice versa, or whether both systems are to be con-

---

bottom (Sialk; all with an estimated volume of ca. 0.5 l) will have served as the concrete objects behind the pictogram ⌇⌇. Since however the strength of the beer is not known, this information is of limited value.

[87]Cf. the commentary below to TY 11 with fn. 153.

[88]Cf. also our remarks below, fn. 159, concerning the possibility that the sign ⌇⌇ would closely correspond to a Mesopotamian surface measure iku, assuming the proto-elamite grain measures were *twice* as large as the proto-cuneiform.

[89]Two texts known to us record a relationship of just 1 ⌇⌇ per ⌇⌇ or ⌇⌇ (*MDP* 6, 399 and *MDP* 26S, 4755), while the text TY 12 may point to a *daily* ration for the worker category ⌇⌇ of 1 ⌇⌇, which may be expected to correspond to the same amount disbursed daily in beveled-rim bowls in Mesopotamia. These relationships thus demonstrate the complexity to be dealt with in the proto-elamite sources and serve as a caveat for readers that all absolute sizes determined for ancient measures are to be recorded *cum grano salis*.

[90]That is, the sign representing one "BUR$_3$", ●, impressed into the center of the larger sign ●.

[91]Cf. our remarks in *ATU* 2, 142.

sidered derivations from a common Near Eastern counting system in part evidenced in the use of preliterate tokens. The evidence at our disposal suggests that the first alternative is the most likely. As already noted by J. Friberg,[92] the linearization of the small values of the proto-elamite ŠE system is suggestive of a development from the more complex proto-cuneiform ŠE system. An apparent increased use of ideographic (or even syllabic) values of numerical signs[93] by proto-elamite scribes can be interpreted as indicating a later stage in the development from iconic to symbolic representation. Finally, the use of the bisexagesimal sign ⧖ with the value 1,000 in the proto-elamite decimal system offers a further argument that a conscious borrowing has taken place. This sign is probably originally derived from two signs ⌓ representing two times sixty. Its use in the decimal system with an entirely different value suggests that the decimal system was a later addition to the proto-cuneiform numerical systems.

Numerical sign systems in the Tepe Yahya texts

We have chosen above a full representation of the Susa numerical systems to aid in the interpretation of the texts from Tepe Yahya, since these few texts registered only comparatively small quantities. A full reconstruction of the systems based on the Yahya sources alone would scarcely have been possible. On the other hand, the understanding of the proto-elamite numerical systems is, because of their specific areas of application, helpful to understand the contents of the Yahya tablets.

In all those cases in which a given notation contains only the signs ▭ and/or ● repeated five times or less, context alone allows of a more specific identification of the numerical system to which the signs belong. With the exception of the ŠE system, no signs above ● are attested in Tepe Yahya; it is thus impossible to identify with certainty the sexagesimal or bisexagesimal system.

Notations from the following texts belong either to the sexagesimal, bisexagesimal or decimal system: all notations in text TY 8, the first notation in TY 12 and all notations in TY 11 and 13.

The notation 8 ▭ in text TY 8, qualified by the sign ●⋖, is possibly a notation in the decimal system. Assuming the logogram is identical with the sign ●⋖ from Susa and the sign ●⋜ from Tepe Sialk, it can be inferred from the entry ●⋜ 2 ▱ [ ] in the text *MDP* 26, 229,[94] and the summation to 1 ▱ 3 ● 1 ▭ of entries including notations qualified by ●⋜ in the text R. Girshman, *RA* 31, 116, that the sign ●⋖ is used with the decimal sys-

---

[92]*ERBM* I, 12-36 and esp. 41-42.

[93]In particular the signs ⌐ (as personal name or object designation in TY 6; passim in the Susa texts, with a number of graphic variants, for which compare *MDP* 31, sign nos. 5175-5185, 5305-5355, and in particular *MDP* 17, 95; *MDP* 26, 216), ⊿ , ⊞ and ⊒ (for instance ⌐⊞ in TY 11; ⊒ ● ● in *MDP* 6, 4994, 4996; *MDP* 17, 139; *MDP* 26, 52, 329; *MDP* 26S, 5045, 5196, 5206-5207 and 5218; PN).

[94]Cp. also the entry ●⋖ 6 ● 1 ▭ in *MDP* 17, 241.

tem.[95] The sign ▭ together with ◇ on the reverse of the same Yahya tablet TY 8 should be classified as a unit of the sexagesimal system, again based on analogy of the sign with other signs which are counted sexagesimally.[96]

The first entry in text TY 12 consists of the sign ≫ together with the decimal notation 3 ● 6 ▭. As will be elaborated in the commentaries to the texts TY 11-13, we interpret the signs ≫ and ⇥ to be designations of humans corresponding to the proto-cuneiform signs SAL (▷) and KUR (⬦) with the possible meaning "female/male slave or low-ranking worker."[97] According to the text *MDP* 26, 205, both signs ≫ and ⇥ were used together with decimal notations,[98] as were all signs probably denoting domesticated animals.

All notations in text TY 11 are notations qualified by ⬦, which is used in the proto-elamite corpus together with decimal notations;[99] there is thus no reason to doubt that these notations are decimal as well, even though no notation on the tablet would of itself allow of a certain identification. The text fragment TY 13 contains only units ▭ and signs which seem to designate persons, so that no more can be said about the numerical system involved than that it will not have been the ŠE system, since one should expect in at least one of the several numerical notations the inclusion of a unit smaller than ▭. The text fragment TY 26, on which no ideogram is preserved, allows of no identification.

All other notations in the texts, including all notations in TY 1-7, 10, the second and third notations in TY 12, and all notations in TY 14-23 and 25, are notations in the ŠE system Š or the derived system Š#. This identification of the employed numerical systems is in most cases already clear from the appearance in the notations of signs specific to the ŠE system. Most notations without such specific signs, i.e., the first notation of text TY 1, the second of TY 3, the two simple units ▭ in TY 14, and the notations in TY 15, 19 and 25, seem clear ŠE notations judging from their respective contexts, however alternative explanations for these notations are offered in the commentaries to the respective texts. The remaining notations 2 ● in TY 10 and 6 ● in TY 16 belong in all probability also to the ŠE system, for which see the commentaries below.

Most of the Tepe Yahya texts may thus be classified alone on the basis of their respective

---

[95]The text *MDP* 17, 394, has a sign very much closer to the signform ● which in copy seems to have been qualified by a sexagesimal notation 2 ▷ [ ]; collation of the original provides, however, a reading 2 ▷ [ ] (the copies in this volume attach no particular importance to the relative size of numerical impressions; cp. text no. 86, with ▷ copied as if it were ▶).

[96]We interpret the sign as a compositum of the signs ◇ and ●, whereby numerical notations like ● inscribed in ▷ signify the amount of grain necessary for the production of one unit of the object ◇. Compare J. Friberg's convincing interpretation of the text *MDP* 17, 171, in *ERBM* I, 34-36, as well as the apparent calculation of 3 ─ from 5 ▭ (= 2 1/2 ─) plus ▭ (= 1/2 ─; both of the questionable signs are damaged) in the text *MDP* 17, 215. Such composita are registered in texts in close connection with the sign ◇ (cp. *MDP* 17, 35), which according to texts cited below, fn. 142, seems to be an object counted with the sexagesimal system. The sign ◇, as is usually assumed, probably corresponded to the proto-cuneiform sign DUG. DUG, furthermore, was in the archaic corpus always used with notations in the sexagesimal system. We therefore suspect that all variants and composita of the sign ◇ were used with the sexagesimal system in proto-elamite texts.

[97]Cp. also our remarks above to the decimal system.

[98]Cp. the text *MDP* 17, 45, with the sign ▷ used with decimal notations.

[99]Cp. for instance *MDP* 6, 317; *MDP* 17, 275-277, 458; and *MDP* 26, 133.

numerical systems. The great bulk of the texts are concerned with grain; one text (TY 12) establishes a relation between decimally counted $>$ and grain measures, another (TY 11) exhibits a certainly decimal count of the object ⬥, and some fragments cannot be assigned with certainty to one of these groups.

There seem to be two important differences between the ŠE-systems in use in Susa and Yahya, both concerning the smallest members of the Yahya system. The Susa sign ❀ was apparently in the Yahya texts replaced by the simplified sign ◆.[100] In the case of the smallest measure, the Susa sign ⬟ (= 1/24 ◠) seems to have been replaced by one or both of two signs in the Yahya corpus, namely, the form ▥ attested in TY 14 and 20 or its apparent inversum ▤ in TY 17.[101] These differences may be understood as evidence for the assumption that the script in conventionalized use in Susa was transmitted to Yahya, where such smallish attacks on graphic conventions were undertaken. This variant system in Yahya

$$\bullet \xleftarrow{10} \bullet \xleftarrow{6} \rhd \xleftarrow{5} \frown \xleftarrow{2} \boxtimes \xleftarrow{3} \text{❀} \xleftarrow{2} \text{◆} \xleftarrow{2} \genfrac{}{}{0pt}{}{▥}{\text{or:}~▤}$$

also contains a simple graphic variant in the form ❀ (= 1/6 $\rhd$) corresponding to the common form ❀ in Susa.[102] The Yahya form corresponds only coincidentally more closely than the Susa form to the sign listed erroneously in *ATU* 2 as the variant ❁ of the more common ❁ (in *ATU* 2: N_{30a-c}) known in proto-cuneiform sources.[103]

TEXTS AND COMMENTARIES

General remarks

Inscribed proto-elamite documents from Tepe Yahya number now 27 tablets, here identified as TY 1-27. The first six tablets treated here as TY 1-6 were published by C. Lamberg-Karlovsky in "Proto-elamite Account Tablets from Tepe Yahya, Southeastern Iran," *Kadmos*

---

[100]This difference was already noted by A. Vaiman, *VDI* 1972:3, 131 with fig. 8.

[101]We are unable to ascertain the exact form of the sign attested in TY 17; according to our photo, there may be no horizontal stroke at the base of that sign. Concerning the peculiar graphic form of the sign ⌐ in TY 20, see our discussion below.

[102]That is, the Susa sign is characterized by the fact that the scribes effected all impressions with the stylus held perpendicular to the surface of the tablet; the central round impression was pressed deeply, the surrounding round impressions lightly into the clay. The same surrounding impressions of corresponding signs in the Yahya texts were made with the stylus held at an angle to the tablet surface. It may be stated in passing that the numerical sign we depict with ▷—as well as sign combinations including this sign—may have been variantly impressed in Susa as in Yahya by first forming its head with the round end of the small stylus; the resulting sign • was then extended to the right by angling the shank of the stylus down into the clay to form the sign •▷.

[103]Cf. *ATU* 2, 138. See the reference above, fn. 84, to the recently auctioned tablet from the Erlenmeyer collection which made possible the arithmetical determination of this sign's value as representing 1/10th the quantity of grain represented by the sign N_{39}.

10 (1971) 97-99 and *Iran* 9 (1971) 89 as nos. 1-6,[104] TY 7 and 8 in id., *Iran* 10 (1972) 98 as E and D; photographs or preliminary copies of most of the other tablets were in turn published by Lamberg-Karlovsky in *Proceedings of the IVth Annual Symposium on Archaeological Research in Iran* (Teheran 1976) 81 and photo 7[105] and, together with M. Tosi, in *East and West* 23 (1973) Figs. 104g and 111-112.[106] We wish to underline the fact that we have not seen the original tablets and so have based our discussion and indeed our own text copies published in the present volume on an analysis of the excavation copies and tablet photographs; the two have in many cases complemented each other, acting to exclude doubts about particular signs and thus resulting in, as we believe, reliable readings. In the case of reverse sides which were neither copied nor photographed during excavations, we have generally assumed that they were uninscribed, without making this explicit in our commentaries below. Impressions of cylinder seals on the tablets[107] will be dealt with in *Excavations at Tepe Yahya: The Third Millennium*, edited by C. Lamberg-Karlovsky and D. Potts (forthcoming).

Given the present stage of decipherment, it seems to us the most reasonable approach to text analysis to classify the proto-elamite texts into categories of content. The categories are dictated, in the first place, by the numerical sign systems prevailing in the particular texts, inasmuch as the numerical notations are sufficiently preserved to allow of clear system ascription. In the second place—for example in those cases in which numerical notations are too damaged or simply too limited to justify their ascription to a numerical system—this categorization must be undertaken by the analysis of ideograms which seem to stand in a particular relationship to numerical sign systems and which thus may be taken as indicators of a particular category such as the account of discrete objects or of grain measures. We have used this latter method of text categorization with some success as a first step in our work on the proto-cuneiform corpus from Mesopotamia, presented as a separate chapter in the revised Uruk Signlist,[108] and believe that its use should precede any further serious work on the proto-elamite text corpus.

As will become clear shortly, the large bulk of the Yahya texts (21 of 27) is concerned with the measurement of quantities of grain. Many of the booked quantities rest within a span which would suggest their identification with rations, i.e., quantities which according to our proposals above under the ŠE system would be sufficient to feed a worker for 1 to 30 days. Other grain quantities, in particular those in connection with the sign ●, might be more compatible with an interpretation as disbursements to groups of individuals, either for their own use or, to name but one possibility, for the sowing of a field of implicit size. Still other texts book with notations incorporating the sign ● grain quantities so large as to suggest a con-

---

[104]See the obverse of TY 1 and 3 with photos in id., "An Early City in Iran," *Scientific American* 224/6 (June 1971) 108. The text published in photo as no. "0" in *Iran* 9, pl. III is our TY 27.

[105]A concordance of the texts in fig. 3, p. 81, with the publication numbers here is as follows: A = (TY) 23, B = 22, C = 19, D = 18, E = 15, F = 12, G = 17, H = 20, I = 16, J = 21, K = 25, L = 26, M = 14, N = 11, O = 13. Photo 7 includes TY 11, 13 and 14.

[106]Figures 111-112 include the obverse and reverse of the texts here published as TY 7-10.

[107]Cf. for example that of TY 23, with sketch in *Proceedings of the IVth Annual Symposium on Archaeological Research in Iran*, p. 81, fig. 3A.

[108]*ATU* 2, chapter 3, pp. 117-166.

nection with disbursements to a large number of individuals or possibly with the accounting of a harvest.[109]

A substantially smaller percentage of the Yahya texts (4 of 27) is concerned with counted objects. Three of these texts seem to record numbers of animals, which we have interpreted to be domestic small cattle (either both sheep and goats, or only sheep). In the case of TY 11, smallish groups of these animals seem either to have been placed in the charge of, or are in some other fashion connected with explicitly named persons.[110]

Only one text (TY 12) seems to explicitly record a number of persons (female workers ?) together with, as we suspect, the quantity of grain they received in one day. See below for a preliminary discussion of this phenomenon, which we were able to document in use in the Susa corpus and which should, beyond its cultural-historical significance, tell us something about the absolute size of grain measures in use in archaic Elam.

Texts concerning cereals

The text Tepe Yahya 1

The obverse of the text is composed of a heading, the "hairy triangle,"[111] followed by six entries. The first five entries consist of a combination of ideographic and numerical notations; the final entry is, on the contrary, comprised of only a numerical notation. All six entries seem according to our reconstruction to have been added together for the total on the reverse.

All ideograms with the exception of 》》》》— and ☞▨ can be identified with signs attested in other cereal texts of the Yahya corpus. The two exceptions appear only on this tablet. The first sign 》》》》— is graphically clear and bears a strong resemblance to the proto-cuneiform sign ŠE, meaning barley or in general grain, however we are unable to document a comparable use of this sign in proto-elamite documents and consider it unlikely, based on the exceedingly few occurrences of the sign, that.it should have represented the common head of grain. The second sign ☞▨ allows of no satisfactory graphical identification based on photos and the copy available to us (the sign is perhaps to be equated with a counted object (?) in *MDP* 26, 201: ☞▨ 1 ● / ◳ 2 ⬦ 2 ◠ 1 ◲).

We assume that all numerical notations except the notation of the second entry (obverse 3) belong to the system Š. Only the initial entry 2 ⬦ is on this point debatable, but seems based

---

[109]A reasonable alternative to this interpretation is of course that, the same as in contemporaneous proto-cuneiform documents, the disbursements to fewer individuals of numerous rationing periods were recorded in a text resembling a general account.

[110]Unclear is the counted object in text TY 13; since it seems that only names of persons are recorded in the preserved section of the text, whose heading is missing, it will probably have to do either with those persons directly, or with objects, in which case probably animals, assigned to them. The latter interpretation is not unlikely, since the persons involved were in several cases the same as those appearing in text TY 11, which registers counted ⊦ ("small cattle" ?).

[111]The sign was discussed above under semantical hierarchy; this is the form with an inscribed tri- instead of the normal Susian quadrilobe. It may be expected that the triangle itself is a general designation for a (productive ?) unit of the proto-elamite administration, the inscribed sign a qualification of specific units.

on the text TY 3 discussed below best interpretable as a grain notation. We shall present directly grounds for alternative interpretations of this notation. The second entry appears to be a clumsy notation in system Š#, for which see the graphically comparable notations in TY 3, 7, 20-21 and in the Susa texts *MDP* 26, 170, 372, 402 and 441, as well as our comments in *ATU* 2, 139 on the same phenomenon in grain notations from archaic Uruk.[112] The derived

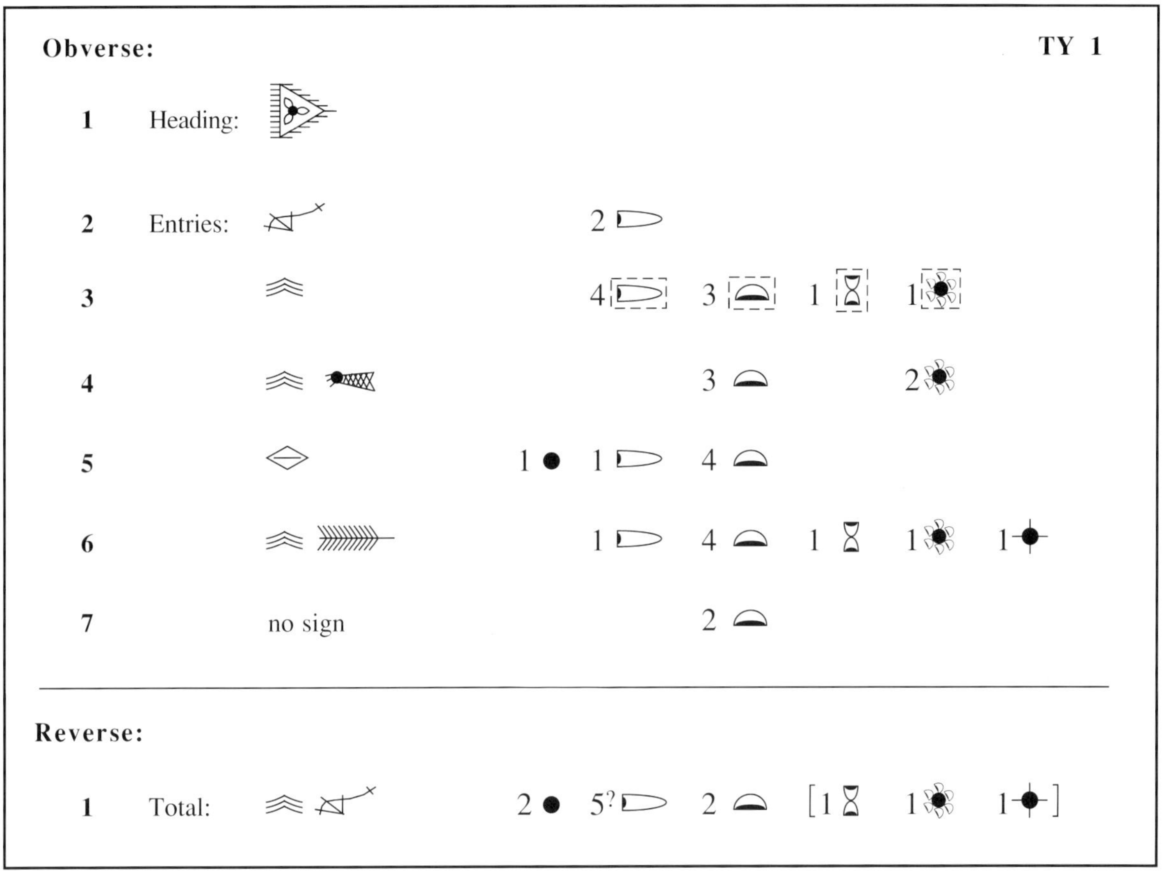

Figure 8. Transliteration of TY 1.

grain notation has apparently here as well as in TY 7 been subsumed in a total written with the standard notational grain system Š. This procedure is ambivalently documented in the Susa texts: *MDP* 26, 48 for instance adds together notations in Š and Š#; the two systems are kept separate in the totals of *MDP* 17, 76, 228 and 243-244, as well as *MDP* 26, 304 and 311. The addition of notations in derived grain systems is on the other hand very well attested in the archaic sources from Mesopotamia.[113]

Our reconstruction of the poorly preserved total must be considered tentative. It would have to assume that the seeming notation 3 ▭ is in fact a damaged 5 ▭ and that the smaller values are completely broken away. A notation 3 ▭ could however be defended by assuming alternatively that the first entry qualified by the ideogram ⊿ˣ is not included in the

---

[112]Cf. the exemplary texts W20044,37 (*ATU* 2, pl. 57; system Š*) and *ATU* 1, no. 285 (system Š").

[113]Cf. our remarks in *ATU* 2, 139-141.

total, similar to TY 2, the entries in which qualified by ⊐ ◇ and ≋ are included in different totals, and supported by TY 19 with entries qualified by ⪤ and by ≋ ⪤ without being totaled.[114] This is a by no means overly speculative explanation, since we know from a large number of Susa texts that the sign ⪤, which is generally identified with the proto-cuneiform pictogram APIN ("plow"), can be qualified by numerical notations in either the sexagesimal[115] or the ŠE-system. When it is quantified sexagesimally, the object ⪤ is often followed by an entry comprised of the ideogram ⧄ and a grain notation. This grain notation invariably expresses a measure of grain equal to 2 ⌒ per ⪤. The sign ⪤ is as a rule qualified by the sign ⧄ when it is followed by a numerical notation in the ŠE system;[116] in those cases where ⪤ is not otherwise qualified and is followed by a grain notation,[117] we assume that an amount of grain is meant which corresponds to a known number or fraction of ⪤.

The interpretation that the numerical notation following the first entry of the obverse of TY 1 is not included in the total would imply that the qualification of the total by the two signs ≋ and ⪤ does not indicate that it is composed of entries qualified by the two signs separately, which is a common method of qualifying summations in proto-cuneiform texts from Mesopotamia. It should furthermore be added that, if the first entry is not included in the total, nothing can be inferred about the system of its numerical notation beyond the fact that it should be either sexagesimal or ŠE. Another alternative would be that the notation 3 ▭ instead of 5 ▭ is simply the result of a scribal error.

The text Tepe Yahya 2

TY 2 is the first of seven texts for which we can determine no certain heading. It seems rather that the first signs represent an initial entry consisting of an ideographic and a numerical notation. We consider this an ideographic notation introducing an individual entry and not a heading because the first two signs ⊐ and ◇ of the composition qualify the first total on the reverse; the third sign ⪤ is often a general qualifier of cereal notations, and in this case may serve to qualify the object ⊐ ◇; it can here just the same not be ruled out that the initial sign ⊐ is in fact a text heading, in which case the ideographic notation of the first entry would begin with the sign ◇. The remaining seven entries of the obverse, which have been added together with the initial entry for the first of two totals on the reverse, are qualified either by no sign, so that their separation into distinct entries must be based on an inconsequence in the numerical notations, or by the stroke "——". It seems that this stroke is only

---

[114]Compare in this regard also the Susa text *MDP* 26S, 4782 (collated), with the apparent addition (obv.) ⌒ ❋ + ⌒ ❋ + ⌒ ❋ = (rev.) 3 ⌒ ▯, excluding the final entry of the obv. ▯ sic ▭.

[115]Compare the sexagesimal notations in the texts *MDP* 17, 413 and *MDP* 26, 103. In the first text as well as in *MDP* 26, 117 and 174 the numerical notations qualifying ⪤ include the sign ⌒, representing "1/2" ⪤. Such notations caution against the conventional translation "plow" of this pictogram. For our interpretation of the sign as a possible surface measure see fn. 159 in the commentary below to TY 11.

[116]Cf. the texts *MDP* 6, 217, 221, 389; *MDP* 17, 18, 54, 126, 127 and 195.

[117]Cf. the Yahya texts TY 2-5 and 19 discussed below with ⪤ followed by grain notations.

used when the preceding numerical notation (in both cases 3 ◠) could not otherwise have been recognized as a distinct entry, for which compare TY 5; the same sign is however in other contexts attested with likely ideographic usage. The initial entry may thus represent a form of text information, which we might call a "subheading," to be hierarchically ordered between a global heading and an individual entry; it qualifies implicitly all save the last of the individual entries of the obverse. The ninth entry qualified by the sign ⩾[118] is repeated as a separate total on the reverse.

All numerical notations are unquestionably in the ŠE system. The text is our most instructive attestation of the numerical structure of this system in Yahya; it implies a summation

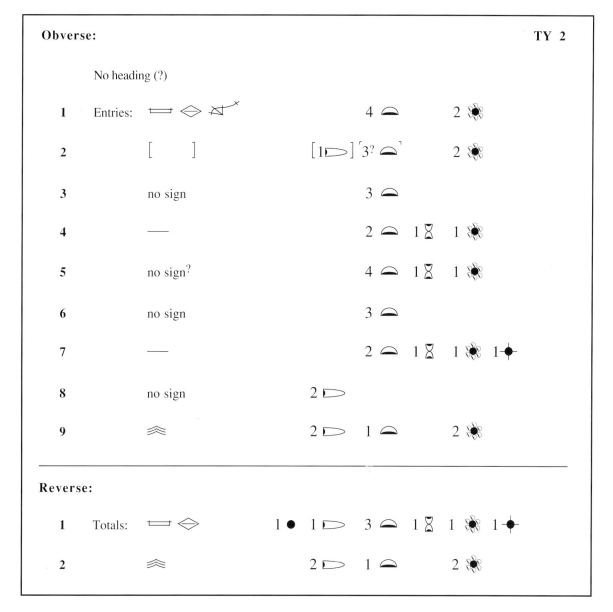

Figure 9. Transliteration of TY 2.

---

[118]Cp. our remarks to TY 1.

which is in perfect agreement with the numerical relationships between the corresponding Uruk and Susa numerical signs, namely:

$$2 \, \triangleright + 18 \, \frown + 2 \, \mathbb{Z} + 6 \, \circledast = 1 \, \bullet.$$

Thus, the text gives a reasonable confirmation of the following relationships:

$$\bullet \xleftarrow{6} \triangleright \xleftarrow{5} \frown \xleftarrow{2} \mathbb{Z} \xleftarrow{3} \circledast {}^{119}$$

The "weak link" in our reconstruction of the text is clearly the second entry; the proposed damaged notation ⌜1 ▷ 3 ⌒⌝ can unfortunately be realized only with substantial, albeit defensible, violence to both copy and photo. It requires a collation of the original in the Teheran museum.

The purpose of separate totals is not apparent in the Yahya corpus; the same phenomenon is common in the Susa texts, and must be the topic of a broader study.

The text Tepe Yahya 3

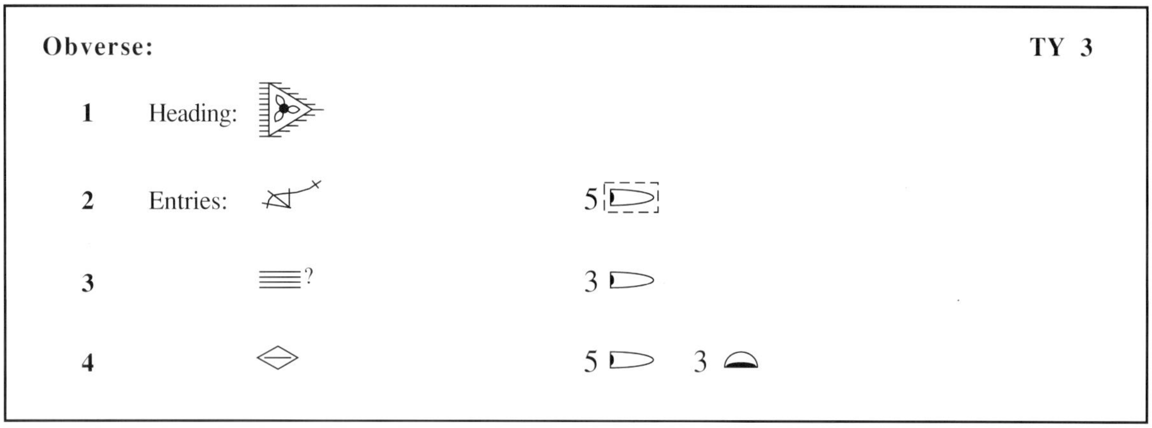

Figure 10. Transliteration of TY 3.

Three entries comprised of ideographic and numerical notations follow the heading ▨ of this cereal text, whose reverse is uninscribed. The four ideograms in this text may be compared with the sequence of heading and ideographic notations in the text TY 1; indeed there the ideographic sequence ⊲⌐ˣ, ≋ and ⬦ corresponds to the sequence ⊲⌐ˣ, ≡ and ⬦ in TY 4, so that the signs ≋ and ≡ may be simple sign variants. The numerical notation in

---

[119]This summation does not prove these relationships, however, since it also allows for diverging numerical solutions. We have analyzed the text by the methods described in *ATU* 2, p. 155, fn. 71. Assuming the reconstruction of the second entry is correct, four solutions which are incompatible with the relations known from the Susa corpus are formally possible. None of the four offers, however, an acceptable alternative to our interpretation. For instance, the following numerical solution of the equation implied by the summation of the text

$$\bullet \xleftarrow{3} \triangleright \xleftarrow{19} \frown \xleftarrow{3} \mathbb{Z} \xleftarrow{6} \circledast$$

is formally possible, but contradicts all numerical relations attested in the Susa texts and moreover contains the extremely unlikely factor 19 between the quantities represented by two consecutive signs.

the system Š# following the first ideogram 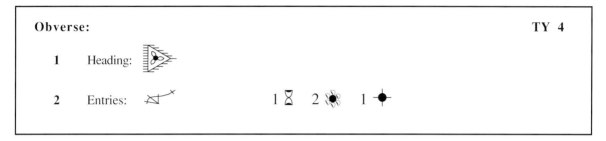 supports the interpretation that the corresponding notation in TY 1 was also, at the least, a grain notation, although possibly not included in the total on the reverse of the tablet.

The text Tepe Yahya 4

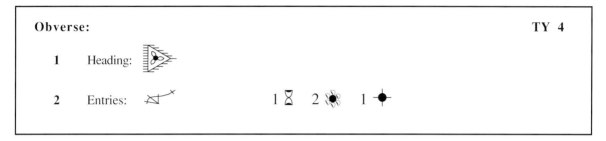

Figure 11. Transliteration of TY 4.

The simple text TY 4, inscribed only on the obverse, consists of the heading ◢▷▷ followed by one entry. The entry is qualified by the same sign ◁╌ which we have seen also in this position in TY 1 through 3. The fact that the following grain notation is just 1/12 ◠ (◆) below ◠ might be of administrative significance.

The text Tepe Yahya 5

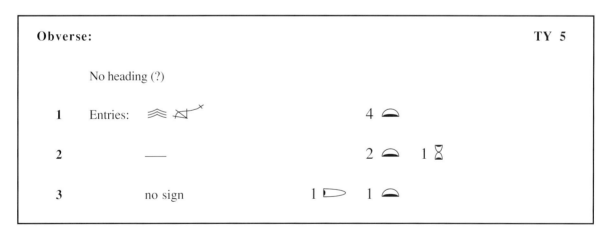

Figure 12. Transliteration of TY 5.

TY 5 seems to have had no text heading, but rather an initial ideographic notation consisting of the signs ≋ and ◁╌; ◁╌ is in this case as in TY 2 the final sign in an initial sign combination.[120] There follow two entries without apparent ideographic notations; the first is merely kept distinct from the second by the separating stroke — since, as we have seen, the

---

[120]There seems according to our photo to have been an erased numbersign — between ≋ and ◁ .

numbersigns ⌒ would otherwise have merged into the inconsistent numerical notation 6 ⌒.[121] The final entry consists entirely of a numerical notation; a dividing stroke is superfluous due to the impossible sign sequence ⚥ ▭ in the ŠE system. The use of the "column" change to signal a new entry seems unlikely, since the text TY 25 has at the beginning of the second "column" the stroke ——, which we assume was used to separate otherwise indistinguishable numerical notations. In fact, the proto-elamite scribes seemed to sense the distinguishing possibilities of the columns only in technical contexts; they refused, for instance, to divide a notation in the system Š# into two parts. Confer for example the space left vacant at the bottom of the first "column" in TY 21, doubtless the result of the scribe's realization that he could not accommodate the following Š# notation in the space remaining. Numerical notations without qualifying ideograms seem to us to imply that all such entries were associated with the initial ideographic notation.

The text Tepe Yahya 6

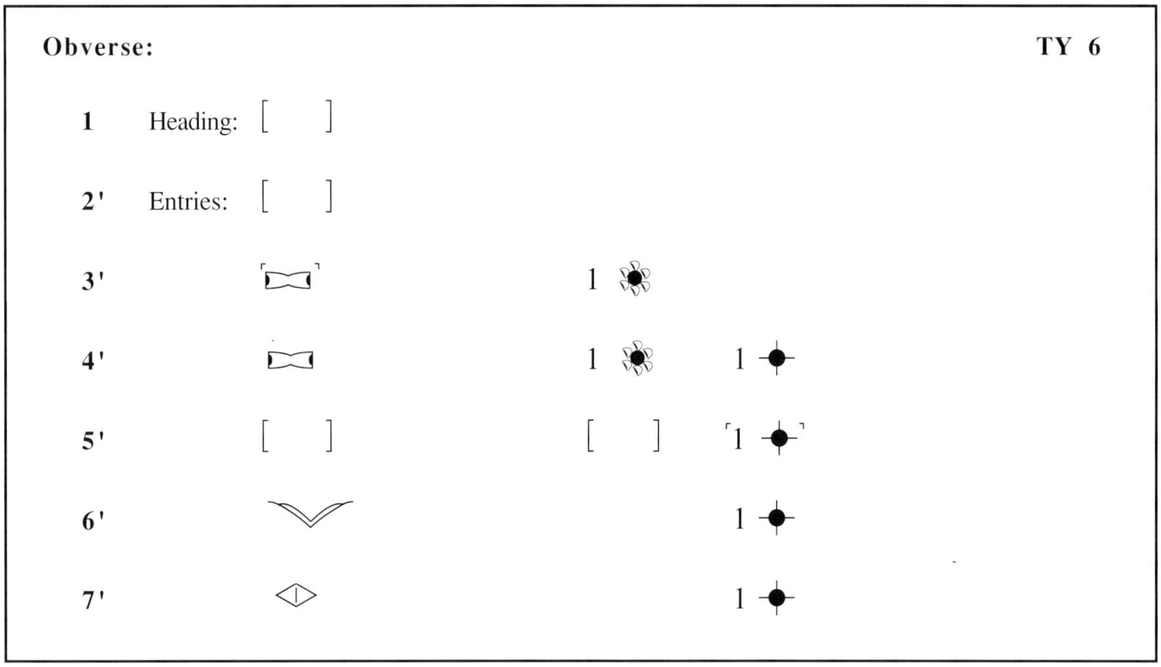

Figure 13. Transliteration of TY 6.

Only the lower half of the TY 6 is preserved, so that a text heading, if there was one, is missing. Preserved are on the obverse five entries, of which four have discernable ideographic notations, each followed by numerical notations representing small amounts of grain. The text might thus record the disbursement of rations for one day to individuals represented by the ideograms initiating each entry.

The first two entries are introduced by the ideogram ▭, which is not uncommon in sim-

---

[121]Inconsistent because 5 ⌒ were in archaic numeration bundled together in the sign ▭.

ilar context in the Susa corpus.[122] It cannot be determined, based on the sign attestations known to us, whether its ideographic usage is related to its numerical usage, equal to 100 of the units ⊂⊃ in the proto-elamite decimal system; nor is the relationship between this ideogram and the at least graphically related signforms ▱, ▨ and ●—● decipherable. The fourth preserved entry ⌣ seems to be a rather clumsy rendering of the sign ⋀⋁, to whose use together with ⧓ and ⫤ as a qualifier in the Susa corpus of discrete objects governing regular quantities of grain we have made reference above. The final ideogram, in the form of a lozenge (resembling the proto-cuneiform sign ḪI) encasing a single vertical stroke, is otherwise unknown to us.

The text seems to be a clear attestation of the numerical use of the sign ✦ in the system ŠE of the Yahya texts. The evidence from this and other texts makes highly probable the conjecture that in Yahya the sign replaced the more complex sign ✸ [123] with a relative value equal to 1/12 ◠. It might, according to our analysis, represent a quantity of grain on the order of 3/10 liter.

The text Tepe Yahya 7

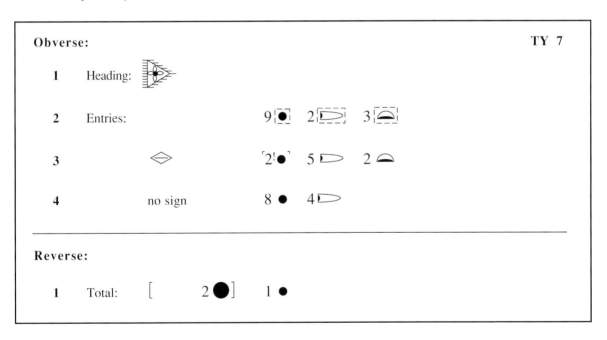

Figure 14. Transliteration of TY 7.

The text consists of a text heading followed by three entries on the obverse, which have, according to our reconstruction, been added together for a total on the reverse. The text heading is the well attested hairy triangle ⧓ inscribed in Susa texts to represent, in all like-

---

[122]Cf. for example grain quantities qualified by ⊏ᵢ in *MDP* 17, 263, 471, *MDP* 26, 439, *MDP* 26S, 4782 and 5241.

[123]See our general discussion above of the numerical sign systems in the Tepe Yahya texts.

lihood, an institutional body. The first entry has no ideographic notation, but is rather an apparently clumsily impressed grain notation in system Š#.[124] The ideographic notation of the second entry is the sign ⬦[125] followed by a grain notation in system ŠE; the final entry follows directly without ideogram and separated from entry 2 only by the discontinuity in the numerical notation.[126] The reconstruction proposed here of the numerical notation in the second entry to the notation ● [+ ●] is based on the presumable total on the reverse of [2 ●] + ● (i.e., 5 ◠ + 11 ▭ + 19 ● = 21 ●). This reconstruction is moreover defensible on the grounds of the alignment and spacing of the numerical signs—it would be unusual to leave space free between first two numerical signs—as well as through an inspection of the photo, which indicates a scuff mark over the space between the first ● and the first ▭'s. Our experience with proto-cuneiform texts is that such scuffings often indicate an uncleaned incrustation, which with an unusual regularity fill the rounded hole left by the impression of ●.

As already indicated, the signs 2 ● of the numerical notation 2 ● 1 ● as well as the ideographic qualification of the total are completely broken away; the break in the tablet is however in conformity with the space requirements of these signs.[127]

The text Tepe Yahya 9

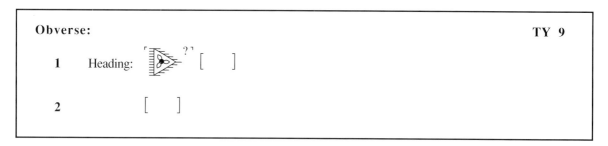

Figure 15. Transliteration of TY 9.

The fragment can be assigned only with reservation to the group of Yahya texts concerning cereals, based on the broken sign , which served there as in Susa as a standard heading for grain texts. The reconstruction of this sign offered seems justified due first to the traces evident on the photo and second to the more common trilobate form in the Yahya texts. Our photos suggest that this fragment, like the following TY 10, was not part of the text TY 7, although all three were from the same locus and TY 9 the same as 10 contains a sign to be expected in the missing part of TY 7.

[124]See our comments above to TY 1. This method of qualifying grain measures must thus assume some of the functions of ideographic notations in the proto-elamite textcorpus.

[125]There was, according to the photo, possibly more than just a horizontal stroke inscribed in the sign. We are unable without collation to offer an exact rendering.

[126]The sign ● cannot represent a grain quantity lower than ◠.

[127]It might in this connection be noted that the corner fragment TY 10, although itself containing the only other Yahya grain notation of this size, indeed exactly 2 ●, and having been unearthed at the same locus as TY 7, cannot, according to the photos available to us, be a part of the text TY 7.

The text Tepe Yahya 10

Figure 16. Transliteration of TY 10.

Although the fragment contains only the remains of a notation 2 ● [   ], there can be little doubt that it was part of a text with large cereal notations; according to the arguments offered above under the ŠE system, this notation would represent ca. 2,880 liters of grain. We have seen that a grain notation of this size is already attested, albeit in damaged context, in the text TY 7. The same notation in the sexagesimal system would represent an unrealistically large quantity[128] and so must be considered highly unlikely; the other possibility, a surface measurement, seems excluded alone by the fact that in the entire proto-elamite corpus but one text[129] evidences the possible use of the corresponding numerical system.

The text Tepe Yahya 14

Following the heading 🏛️ of TY 14 are, depending on the number of signs lost in the broken lower left corner, either 16 or 17 entries, each consisting of ideograms qualifying smallish quantities of grain, i.e., according the the data presented above under the ŠE system, between ▭ ≈ 24 liters and ⬭ (//🏛️ ?) = 1/120 ▭ or ≈ 0,2 liters (?; the final sign might alternatively be interpreted as a quantity of grain measured in the system Š" corresponding to ⬭ in the ŠE system). We therefore assume that the text records the disbursement of rations to persons/officials represented by the ideograms immediately preceding the numerical notations.

It is at present still difficult, as we have stated, to establish clear syntactical rules distinguishing those ideograms which represent persons/officials from those which represent counted objects. This is particularly the case with texts like TY 14, in which a sequence of ideograms known in other contexts to represent counted objects occur interspersed with relatively infrequently or rarely attested signs. The latter would, due to their infrequency and their position in the text, more likely represent persons without official status, such as we might expect in a list of rations.

The second entry consists solely of a numerical notation in system Š#, again, as we have

---

[128]That would be 2 "ŠAR$_2$" = "7200" units. This number would be very much larger than the largest number of discrete units attested in the Yahya corpus.

[129]*MDP* 26S, 5224, from Susa (cf. the discussion above under the GAN$_2$ system).

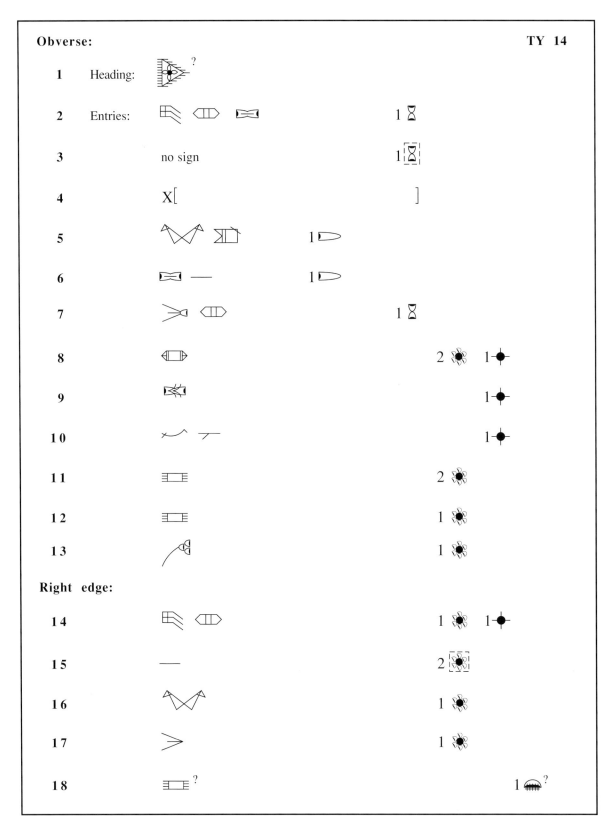

Figure 17. Transliteration of TY 14.

seen in other texts (TY 1, 3 and 7), clumsily drawn. The final entry on the lower right edge consists of an unclear ideogram followed by a seemingly secure attestation of the numbersign ⬛, which we have above interpreted to be, together with a variant form ⬛ in the text TY 17, the sign in Yahya corresponding to the Susa form ⬛. The graphic form of the sign in TY 14 is not entirely clear; the horizontal stroke at the base of the sign may in this case, unlike the clear attestation in TY 20 (see the discussion below), be no more than a scratch on the tablet's surface, and the sign itself, as stated above, a representation of grain measured in the system Š" corresponding to ⬛ in the basic grain system.

The text Tepe Yahya 15

The text TY 15 is to be included with the grain texts due to the presence of the ideogram ⬛, which is the most common qualifier of grain quantities in the proto-elamite text corpus. The numerical notation 2 ⬛ following ⬛ is thus with some likelihood in the system Š. The heading of this text, consisting of two horizontal strokes, is otherwise seldom in the Yahya (only in TY 15 and 18) and Susa corpus.[130] In TY 18 the sign qualifies one of several entries on the obverse, the numerical notations of which are totaled on the reverse and qualified with the sign ⬛, as here. This together with the size of the tablet suggests that TY 15 might be a receipt, along the formal lines of tablet typology known from Mesopotamia; texts like TY 18 would on the other hand correspond to the accounts which were drawn up based on individual receipts and the like.

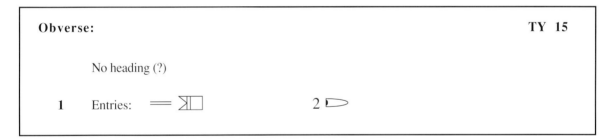

Figure 18. Transliteration of TY 15.

The text Tepe Yahya 16

TY 16 is inscribed only on the obverse, and its inscription seems, despite the chipped upper right corner, to be complete. The initial sign ⬛ of the tablet is well represented as a heading in Susa texts, qualifying measures of grain as well as numbers of decimally counted animals/humans.[131] The central circle of the sign was not inscribed, but rather impressed with, it

---

[130]It is not clear whether the sign can function in numerical as well as in ideographic use; see below, fn. 153.

[131]Together with animals in the texts *MDP* 26, 55 and 225; with humans (and animals?) in *MDP* 26, 51; with grain

seems, the stylus used for the numbersign ●. The same may be assumed for the attestations of this signform from the Susa corpus, although this fact is not obvious from the text copies.

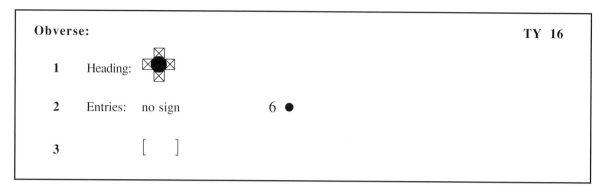

Figure 19. Transliteration of TY 16.

The following numerical notation 6 ● makes the inclusion of this tablet among the grain texts on the whole secure, although other interpretations are defensible. The first alternative would be a notation in the surface area system G(AN$_2$), for which there is however precious little evidence in the proto-elamite corpus. The second, a notation in the decimal system, may be considered unlikely since these notations are as a rule qualified by ideograms representing the objects being counted. The seeming indentations between the numerical signs (see the copy), moreover, might point to another clumsy rendering of a grain notation in the derived system Š#. On the basis of our photos alone, we are unable to make this determination.

The text Tepe Yahya 17

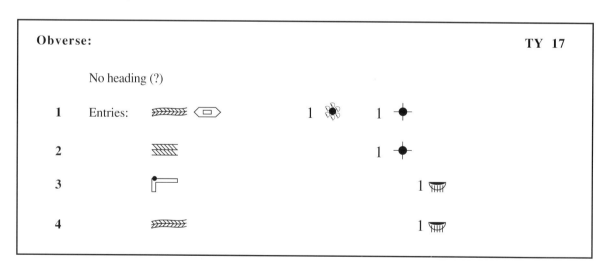

Figure 20. Transliteration of TY 17.

measurements in *MDP* 26, 47, 58-60 and 267. In the last text the sign is attested following an individual entry qualified by the sign ⤳ . The text may thus have been a general account including entries from "institutions" qualified by their respective symbols. The text *MDP* 26, 80 registers probable grain products quantified with the bisexagesimal system; the heading of TY 16 is here as in *MDP* 26, 267 in clear parallelism to the standard heading ⤳ .

The tablet consists of four entries without an apparent heading. Each entry consists of ideographic and numerical notations. Since the numerical notations are of quite small grain quantities, we interpret this text, like TY 6 and 14 above, to be the record of grain disbursements in the form of rations. The ideographic notations might be qualifications of the grain issues, as is clear in the case of the first entry with ⬭, which we know to be the designation of a common grain product and which has been translated by various authors as "bread." They might also be the names or titles of persons receiving grain, since in the case of the last three entries the logograms are exceedingly rare.

The text Tepe Yahya 18

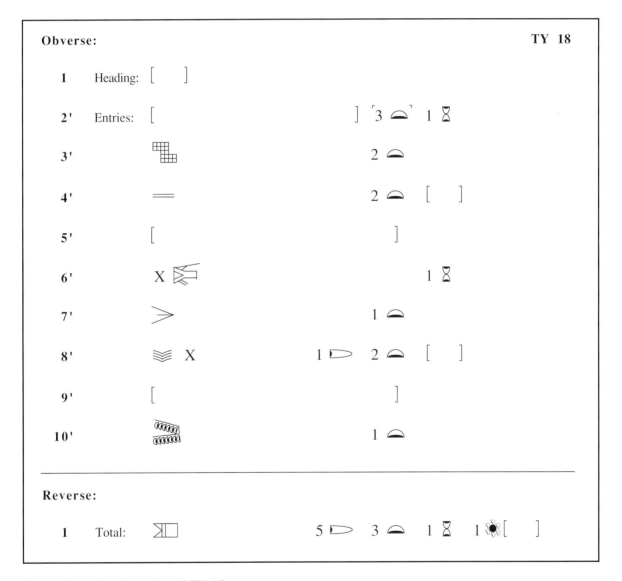

Figure 21. Transliteration of TY 18.

We find in this text support for our interpretation of the sign ✦ as a simplification in Yahya of the sign ✺ common to the Susa corpus, since it not only follows ✺ in the first entry, but in the sequence of four entries, which in other texts is as a rule governed by decreasing grain quantities, assumes a position between ✺ and ▥. The sign ▥ is thus the second very interesting numerical notation in this text, since it seems to be an inverse form of the sign ▦. These two notations and that in TY 20 are our only references from the proto-elamite corpus to this variant form of the sign ▦ attested in Susa.

Both obverse and reverse of TY 18 are inscribed; the reverse contains with high probability the total of the numerical notations of the obverse, an uncertain number of which are broken away. The presumable heading of the obverse is missing together with one or two entries in the first, and probably one or two entries in each of the second and third "columns." The preserved entries are of the standard form, consisting of a notation of one or more ideograms, followed by a numerical notation. All numerical notations are of medium-sized quantities of grain; the quantities seem in any case too large to allow of an identification of the text as a record of daily rations. The ideographic notations are nonetheless very uncommon in proto-elamite texts, suggesting that the text recorded disbursements of some sort to persons represented by the ideograms. The ideogram ══ heading the third preserved entry is likely the same sign used as a tablet heading in TY 15; there also the grain quantity recorded is qualified with the sign ⧄▢, which here qualifies the total of numerical entries on the reverse. The preserved grain notations on the obverse add up to 3 ▷ 1 ▱ 1 ⧗ 1 ✺(?), a sum which makes the notation 5 ▷ 3 ▱ 1 ⧗ 1 ✺ of the reverse a nearly certain candidate to be the total of all entries of the obverse (missing are merely notations totaling 2 ▷ 2 ▱). This total is qualified by the ideogram ⧄▢ (usually believed to correspond to the later Sumerian sign "gur," which was, perhaps parallel to this proto-elamite sign, originally the designation of a large container for cereals).

Since TY 15 seems to have been an individual "receipt" comparable to those known from Mesopotamian sources, TY 18 might represent an account drawn up to consolidate such individual transactions. We have interpreted the ideogram heading the sixth preserved entry, ≻, to be the designation of a female worker of low status.[132] This interpretation suggests that the grain disbursements recorded in TY 18 might have been effected for several individuals noted with a collective designation. The entry ≻ ▱ would thus be translated: "(for the) low-ranking female worker(s): one ▱ (of grain)."

The text Tepe Yahya 19

This puzzling small tablet inscribed on both obverse and reverse appears to record two separate transactions. It seems likely to belong to the grain texts due to the qualification of the the numerical notations on both sides by the signs ⊿ and ≋, which are common ideograms together with grain notations in the Yahya corpus. The heading of the obverse is moreover

---

[132]See our commentary to the texts TY 11-12.

itself in standardized and variant forms normally used to qualify cereal accounts.[133]

We wish to state in passing that there could in fact be a numerical relationship between the notations on the two sides of the tablet; in the ŠE system, the first notation 1 ● 4 ▭ would equal (6 + 4 =) 10 ▭, the second notation 1 ● 3 ▭ would equal (6 + 3 =) 9 ▭, or 10% less than the first. We note this circumstance only because of the multifarious, often unexplained reductions and increases of quantities of grain and other commodities recorded in the texts from Mesopotamia, which we might call "administrative adjustments"[134] until the exact nature of the reductions and increases is understood.

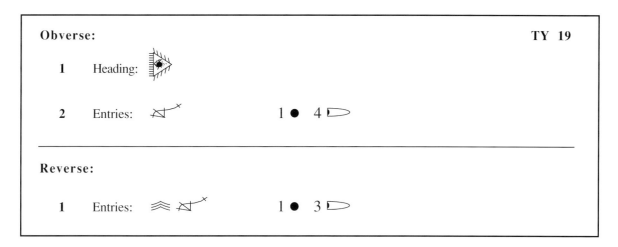

Figure 22. Transliteration of TY 19.

The text Tepe Yahya 20

The text records in 3[+ ?] entries quantities of grain. The first entry is qualified by the sign ≋, which is common in the cereal texts discussed here. We interpret the sign ▥ (with the graphic form ▥; see the discussions of TY 14 and 17) at the end of the first notation as a variant of the smallest unit of grain measure in the Susa ŠE system, ▱. This interpretation of the sign can be defended, first, because the sign would then fit into the numerical sequence of a presumable notation 1 ▭ 1 ⧖ 2 ✸ 1 ▥. Furthermore, the second entry consists of another rather clumsy notation in the system Š#. Comparable notations in the Susa material are very often not qualified by a preceding ideogram (compare here TY 14, 21 and 23). The graphical differences between the signs ▥/▥ and ▱ are, moreover, not large. The scribe has in his rendering of the former sign added at the base of an impressed ◠ a horizontal stroke, from which four vertical bars were drawn. While the Susa form of this sign discussed above under the ŠE system and cited in the Yahya signlist at the end of this chapter[135] does

---

[133]A clumsily drawn tri- or quadrilobe seems to have been inscribed in the triangle.

[134]Cf. R. Englund, *JESHO* 31, 151[27].

[135]See the form cited in *MDP* 31 as no. 4825. The signform is, despite our photo, graphically not entirely clear. We assume that its upper part was impressed with the stylus used for numerical notations, but the photo also allows for the interpretation that the sign was wholly inscribed with the incising end of the stylus. A collation of the original in

not entirely conform with the sign in TY 20, in that instead of vertical strokes below, oblique strokes were drawn above the horizontal, the same sign in the text *MDP* 26, 372 does exhibit this peculiarity. This sign form was not incorporated in the signlist in *MDP* 31. While the signs in both texts *MDP* 26, 372 and 169 (this latter attestation the basis of the form in *MDP* 31) were used ideographically in their respective texts, no analogous ideographic application is likely in the present case. In the cited Susa examples, the sign represented ideographically a measure of grain counted by following notations in the bisexagesimal system; in TY 20, the following notation is itself a grain measure. The final, partially preserved entry in TY 20 is so obliterated as to make its identification impossible.

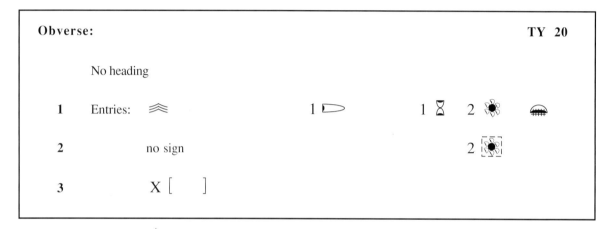

Figure 23. Transliteration of TY 20.

The text Tepe Yahya 21

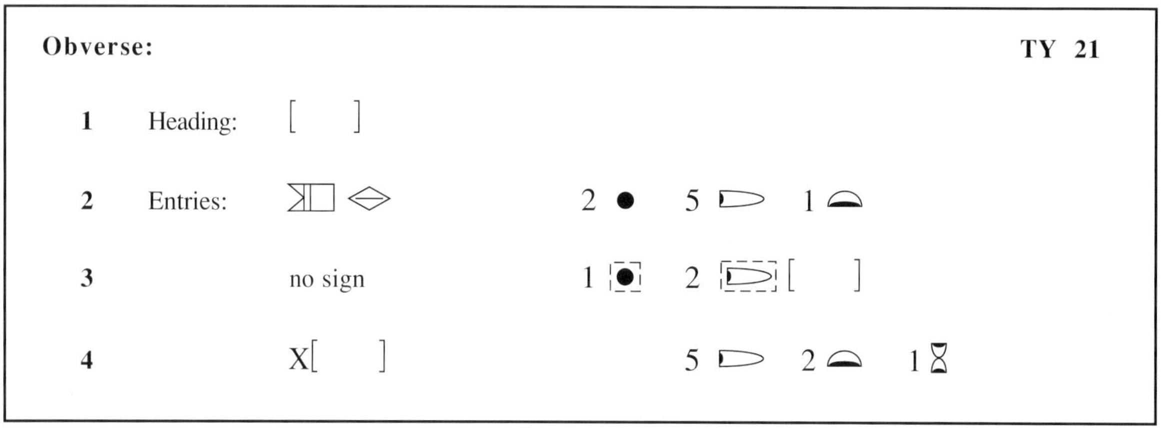

Figure 24. Transliteration of TY 21.

The heading of the tablet TY 21 is broken away. There follow 3 entries, one of which using the system Š# has no ideographic notation. The first entry is qualified by the signs and

the Teheran museum will be necessary to resolve this dilemma.

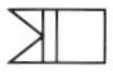

◇, the second of which was in the comparable position of the second of two signs (after ⟺) in TY 2. This sign ◇ alone, however, qualified quantities of grain in both TY 3 and 7 and might thus represent a quantified object or the title of some person or persons. Both TY 3 and 7 contained grain notations in the system Š#; parallel to these texts, another clumsy notation in this system follows here as the second entry, having no ideographic notation. As already stated above, this notation was, due to obvious scribal convention, held together in the second column, thus leaving space vacant in the first. The ideographic notation of the last entry is lost in a break in the tablet.

All numerical notations are of comparable, although decreasing, size. According to our interpretation, the first notation records a grain quantity of ca. 300, the second of ca. 150, the last of ca. 100 liters.

The text Tepe Yahya 22

The heading of the small tablet TY 22 is clearly a damaged ▷, of which the inscribed sign (✦, ✦, etc.) is lost. Two entries follow, both consisting of an ideographic notation and a numerical notation representing small quantities of grain. The first, ∨⟋, is probably an unfinished rendering of the sign ∧⟋; this form is also attested in the text TY 6 and may be a semantically distinguished variant form. The second, ⌐⋈, is in the Yahya texts attested only here; the sign form is perhaps to be included among those signs which are generally considered representations of beer containers.[136] The numerical sign ✹, standing for the amount of grain connected with the object represented by this ideogram, is according to our calculations equal to ca. 0.6 liter.

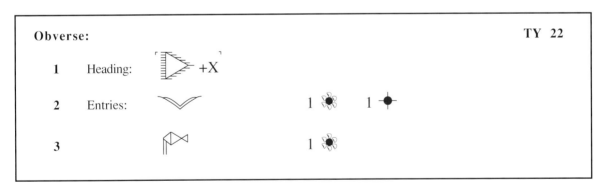

Figure 25. Transliteration of TY 22.

The text Tepe Yahya 23

The tablet TY 23 consists of a heading and two entries on the obverse. Despite apparently substantial damage to the sign, the photo seems to justify our interpretation of the heading as

---

[136]*MDP* 31, 2702ff.; cp. in particular 4157-4194, and the commentary below to TY 8.

the common ideogram ⟦image⟧ in its variant Yahya trilobate form.

The two entries are similar to entries in TY 21: the first contains an ideographical notation including the sign ⟦image⟧ (the same as in TY 21, there with the further qualifying logogram ⟦image⟧) followed by a numerical notation of very nearly the same size as in TY 21; the second apparently contains only a numerical notation in the system Š#. This final notation is however of an unclear form (see photo), for which we are able to cite no parallel references.

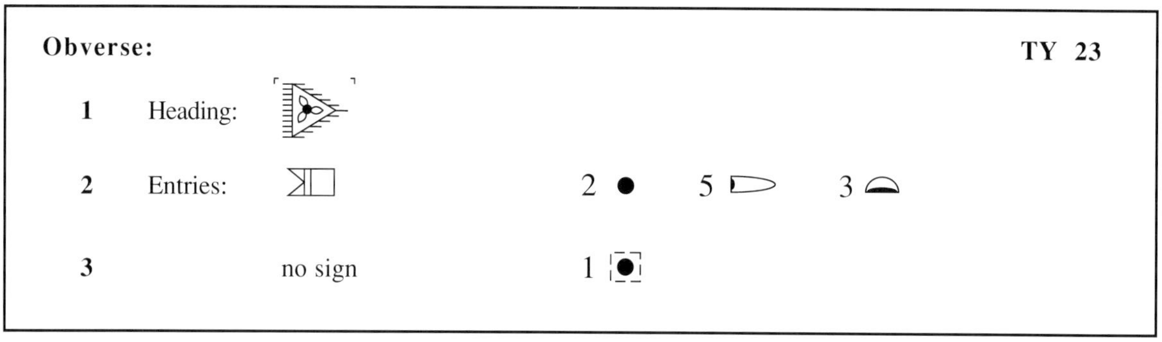

Obverse: **TY 23**

  1   Heading: ⟦image⟧

  2   Entries: ⟦image⟧   2 ●   5 ▷   3 ⌒

  3   no sign   1 ⟦image⟧

Figure 26. Transliteration of TY 23.

The text Tepe Yahya 24

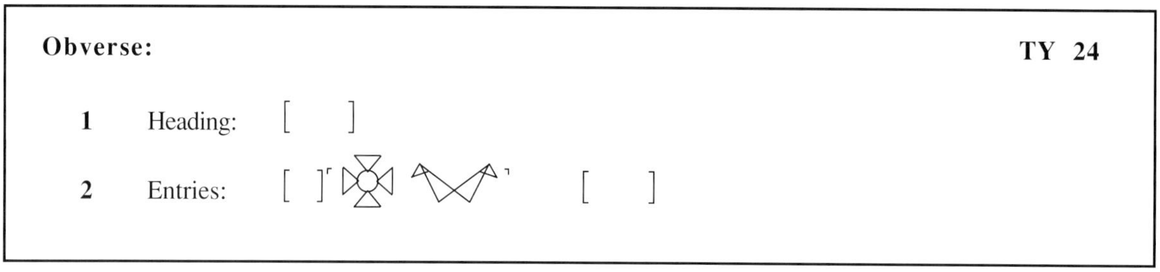

Obverse: **TY 24**

  1   Heading: [   ]

  2   Entries: [ ]⟦image⟧ ⟦image⟧   [   ]

Figure 27. Transliteration of TY 24.

The fragment TY 24 contains no preserved numerical notation; our ascription of the text to the group of grain texts results from an inclusion of the sign ⟦image⟧, which is as a rule here as in Susa directly quantified by or set in relation to measures of grain. Although this sign would thus make defensible the assignation of this tablet to the cereal texts, its appearance in the "animal" text TY 11 recommends caution when in broken context. The first sign in the notation is damaged; we have restored it to ⟦image⟧ (the central circle is etched, and not an impressed ● of the thick "numbers" stylus) based on the symmetry common in proto-elamite signs and on a comparison with the sign ⟦image⟧ (written with ●).

The text Tepe Yahya 25

The final clear cereal text in the Yahya corpus, TY 25, is a fragment consisting of two preserved entries and no apparent heading. The first entry is the common sign used to qualify grain quantities, ⅀⌷, followed by a numerical notation, of which only part of the sign ▻ is preserved. The second entry is only interesting for the clue it gives for the contemporary understanding of tablet and text structure. We have already stated above that the stroke "——" seems to be used to separate otherwise indistinguishable cereal notations which are in sequence without qualifying ideograms. We may suspect here that this stroke is indeed used in this fashion, since the tablet, so far as it is preserved, has only notations including ▻. The use of this graphic separator at the beginning of the second "column" would indicate again that the scribes attached no importance to the "columns" themselves, which is obvious from all larger proto-elamite texts, but rather that they inscribed tablets as if they consisted of one long line. This is a major difference between these texts and the administrative records of Mesopotamia, which still in the latest phase Uruk III are distinguished by an involved hierarchical tablet division.

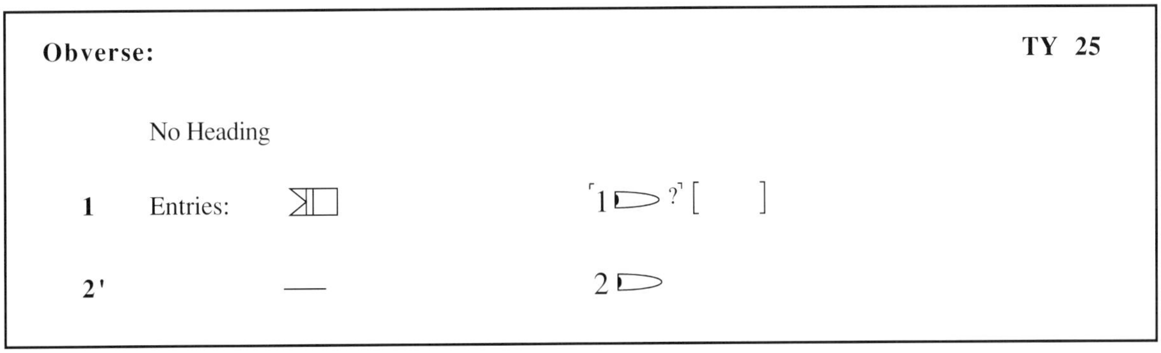

Obverse: **TY 25**

          No Heading

1   Entries: ⅀⌷   ⌈1 ▻ ?⌉ [   ]

2'   ——   2 ▻

Figure 28. Transliteration of TY 25.

Texts concerning counted objects

The text Tepe Yahya 8

TY 8 is the only text in the Yahya corpus with an object designation ●≮ which, in a variant form in sums in Susa texts,[137] can be subsumed under semantic categories represented by the signs ⊕ or ◯≮. Both of the latter signs have plausibly been connected with proto-cuneiform signs clearly designating small cattle (sheep and goats). The sign ●≮ shares itself a strong resemblance with the proto-cuneiform sign for a nanny goat, UD_5 (⊕≮). All objects represented with this sign complex in the proto-elamite texts were qualified with numerical notations in the decimal system. It is therefore to be assumed that the notation 8 ▻ following ●≮ is a notation in this numerical system, denoting 8 such animals.

The entry preserved on the reverse of the tablet, albeit severely damaged, may be determined to be the only probable sexagesimal notation in the Yahya corpus. This identification

---

[137]The usual form is ● ≺ ; the possible variation seems however to be large, for which cf. the signlist *MDP* 31, nos. 5187-5208.

may be cautiously advanced with the following justification. First there is reason to believe that the signs clearly representing jars of beer, that is, those signs in which lower members of the ŠE system were inscribed and which thus seem to signify quantities of beer brewed with a measure of grain corresponding to the encased ŠE notation, were quantified with numerical signs from the sexagesimal system.[138] Since the areas of application of the bisexagesimal system in the proto-elamite corpus seem to correspond to those in proto-cuneiform texts, that is, for the notation of units of dry grain products disbursed as rations,[139] one might expect that the same numerical system would be in use in proto-elamite as in proto-cuneiform texts to qualify units of liquids, namely, the sexagesimal system.[140] Second, numerous texts from

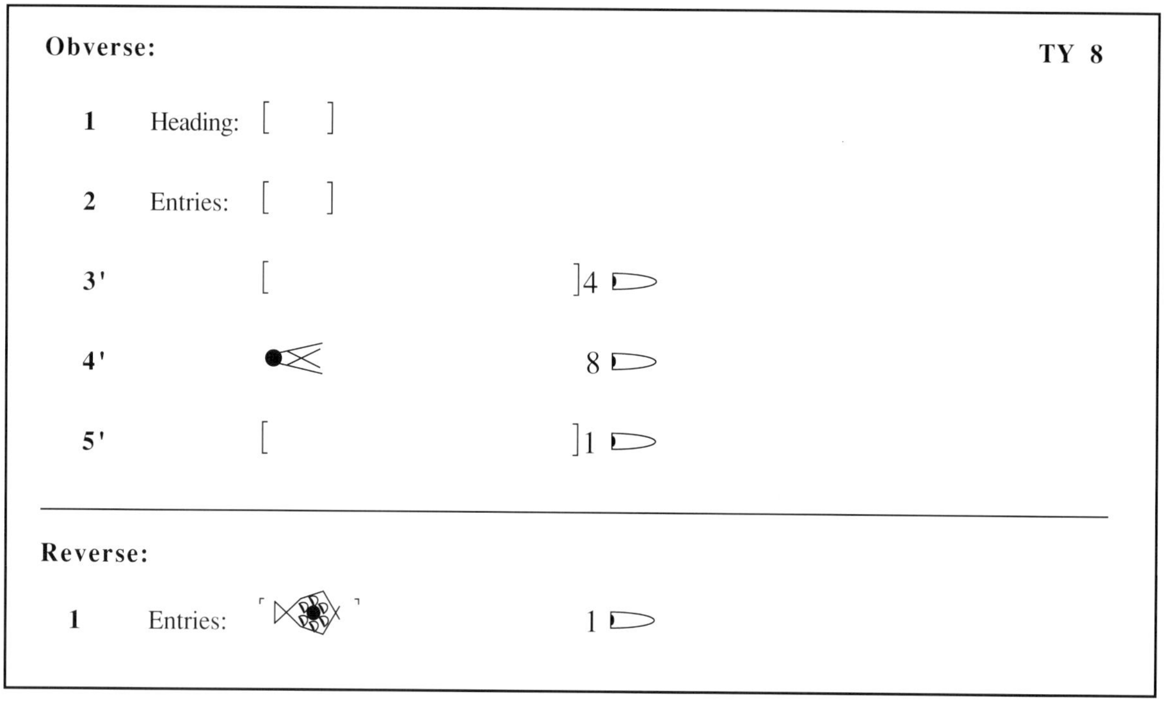

Figure 29. Transliteration of TY 8.

Susa with, instead of the "beer jug," signs such as ⟨symbol⟩ which seem to represent measures of milk products,[141] are qualified with numerical notations which can be plausibly interpreted to be sexagesimal.[142] This indicates that even though we are unable to cite large notations of "beer jugs" which would obviate the necessity of conjecture, the relatedness of ceramic jugs

---

[138]This use may be inferred from the texts *MDP* 6, 211, *MDP* 17, 8, 35, 215, and especially in *MDP* 17, 171, for which cf. J. Friberg, *ERBM* I, 34-36.

[139]See our remarks above to the proto-elamite bisexagesimal system.

[140]Cp. *ATU* 2, 129-130.

[141]Such signs seem to correspond to the signs related to KISIM in the proto-cuneiform corpus; cp. *ATU* 2, loc.cit.

[142]Cf. the proto-elamite texts *MDP* 17, 35, 107; *MDP* 26, 210 and 349. The texts *MDP* 26, 210 and 461 suggest by association the use of ⟨symbol⟩ with sexagesimal notations; ⟨symbol⟩ and related signs seem associated with animal products in the texts *CahDAFI* 1, fig. 58, no. 14, *MDP* 17, 97, 161, and 172; with grain products in *MDP* 17, 133 and 352; *MDP* 26, 132 and 349 (all from Susa).

and the products they contained should result in the use of the same numerical system for all such objects.

The text Tepe Yahya 11

TY 11 is the most complex text among those almost completely preserved texts excavated at Tepe Yahya. After the heading the text contains 17 entries, five of which being partly damaged cannot be completely reconstructed. All entries exhibit the same format, including first an ideographic and then a numerical section. Ideographic notations begin with the sign ⌦ and end with the sign ⬧. The two signs encase one or a combination of signs, most of which appear only once on the tablet.

We interpret the initial sign ⌦ of each entry to denote a special type of low-rank worker, indicating that the following sign or sign combination, which must be a personal name, belongs to this category of workers. The concluding sign ⬧ is conventionally translated "sheep." Numerical notations at the end of each entry are in the decimal system and record for each name a certain number of sheep. The preserved numbers range from 2 (seventh entry) to 32 (third entry). There is no obvious relation between the order of the entries and the numbers of sheep recorded; it will likely have been coincidental that the higher numbers are recorded at the beginning and at the end of the text. The text implies that the listed persons are in some way responsible for keeping or delivering the sheep recorded after their names; we are unable to give any further explanation of the precise relation between the registered persons and the corresponding groups of sheep.

The main sources for this interpretation are close parallels in the proto-elamite text corpus which may favorably be compared to the textual details as well as to the semantical structure of the text as a whole. The closest parallels we could find to the text as a whole are the texts *MDP* 6, 212 and 353. The main difference between both of these texts and the text TY 11 is that in the former only the first name is qualified by the sign ⌦. *MDP* 6, 212 has four entries with numbers of sheep ranging from 9 to 22;[143] *MDP* 6, 353 has seven entries with numbers ranging from one to three sheep and a total on the reverse of 13 sheep.

The sign ⬧ seems exclusively used as a symbol for counted objects. Its own graphic form as well as its association with other signs which bear a strong graphic resemblance to proto-cuneiform signs known to represent domestic animals, in particular small cattle,[144] makes plausible the interpretation of this sign as "sheep." The fact that these signs are on the

---

[143] The final entry is according to collation to be corrected to ⊢ 1 ● 6 ▷; the text, furthermore, has a fully preserved reverse, with the correct summation ⊢ 6 ● 5 ▷.

[144] Compare the signs UDU, U_8, UDUNITA, MAŠ, MAŠNITA, UD_5, etc., in *ATU* 2 s.v., with the proto-elamite signs ⊢, ⋜, ⌀, ⊹, ⊶, ● and ●⋜. Numerous texts document the close affinity of these signs, see for example *MDP* 17, 96-97; *MDP* 26, 216 (with on the reverse a decimal sum of "106+" ⊢) and 217. In the case of *MDP* 26, 176 and 437, moreover, the counted objects ⊢ and ⌀, and ●⟨, ⊢, ⊹ and ●, respectively, seem to be subsumed in totals qualified by the sign ⊢, in exact parallel to the use of the sign UDU in the proto-cuneiform sources to qualify all small cattle (that is, excluding cows [AB_2] and oxen [GU_4]). The semantic consequences of the qualification of numbers of ⊢ and ●⟨ as ⋜ in the total of *MDP* 26, 390, on the other hand, remain unclear to us (read obv.¹ ⊠ ⊢ 5 ▷ [ ]¹2▷¹ ●⟨ 6 ▷ ● ⟨¹ 1 ▷ rev.¹ ⋜ 1 ● 4 ▷).

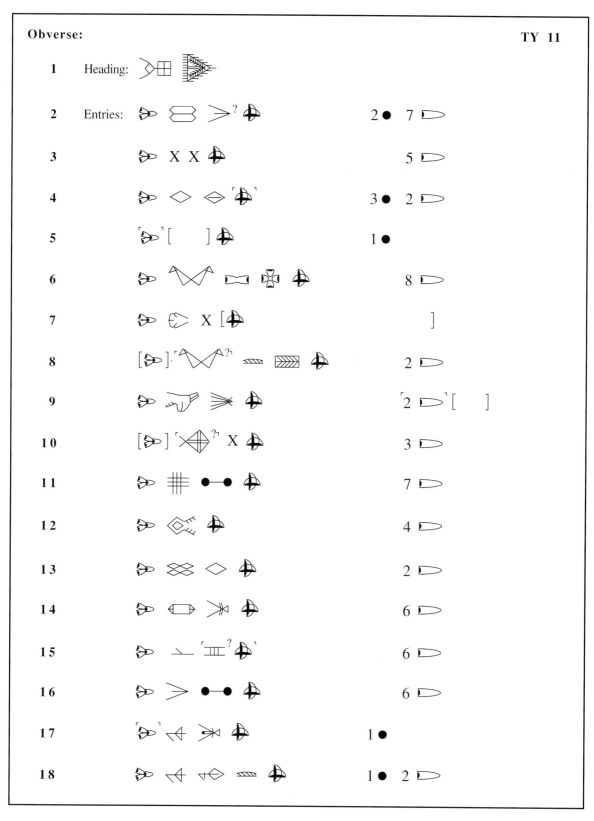

Figure 30. Transliteration of TY 11.

whole abstract forms may be suggestive either of a set of symbols commonly shared in Mesopotamia and Susiana for domestic animals prior to the inception of written documents,[145] or—and this seems to us more likely—of a defective borrowing of signs already in use in Uruk.

A further argument in favor of the interpretation that the sign ⊕ and associated signs represented domestic animals lies in the nature of the essentially rural economy in archaic Persia, namely, that one should expect to find as the major components in administrative documentation of the period produce from grain agriculture and from herds of sheep and goats. The very numerous administrative documents recording often large quantities of grain are known to us from a simple categorization of the texts according to the numerical systems in use. We should expect to find in the texts carrying notations in the numerical systems used to count discrete objects—this use seems beyond reasonable doubt in the case of the sexagesimal and bisexagesimal systems already known from proto-cuneiform sources, as well as in the case of the proto-elamite decimal system—records of the certainly second most important commodity in the proto-elamite (as in the archaic Mesopotamian) society, that is, of caprids and caprid products. The large numerical notations in proto-elamite texts qualified by the ideograms ⊕ and signs related to the ideogram ⊕ seem thus consonant with an identification of these signs with small cattle.[146] This identification is relatively well supported by texts documenting feed for cattle[147]. Finally, it may be added that in a number of cases the contents of texts recording numbers of ⊕ and related signs have been verified with seals which themselves are suggestive of officials connected with the administration of herds of small cattle.[148]

The sign ⊳ (Yahya variant: ⊳) is the most common sign used as a symbol qualifying

---

[145]This plausible interpretation would follow the argumentation of D. Schmandt-Besserat (see the bibliography in this volume for her contributions), who has posited a linear relation between certain clay "tokens" with an incised cross and the proto-cuneiform sign UDU.

[146]Cp. the texts *MDP* 6, 317 (with rev. ⊕ 2 ⊂ 9 • 3 ⊳ = "293 small cattle" [total of ⊕ and +]), *MDP* 17, 275 (with rev. ⊕ 3 ⊂ 1 ⊳ [ ] = "301+ ⊕-small cattle" following the notation ⊰ 1 ⊠ 2 ⊂ [ ] = "1200+ (head of the) ⊰-small cattle(?)"), 276 (with rev. ⊕ 1 ⊂ ⌜6 •⌝ [ ] = "160+ (head of the) ⊕-small cattle" following ⊰ 6 ⊂ 4 • 5 ⊳ = "645 ⊰-small cattle(?)"), *MDP* 26, 133 (with rev. [⊕ 5⊂] 7 • = "570 ⊕-small cattle") and 216 (with rev. ⊕ 1 ⊂ 6 ⊳ [ ] = "106+ ⊕-small cattle"). These notations are in magnitude rivaled only by notations qualified by a complex of signs which we interpret to represent worker categories or possibly work units. Cf. below and the notations as high as 5 ⊂ 9 • 1 ⊳ = "591" (of the category ⊳) in *MDP* 17, 45, 1 ⊠ 7 ⊂ 7 • 4 ⊳ [ ] = "1774+" (of the category ⊳ + ⊳) in *MDP* 26, 205, and 2 ⊠ 5 ⊂ 3 • 1 ⊳ = "2531" (of the category ⋎) in the text *MDP* 26, 156 (the extraordinarily high totals may be of work units, e.g., "X-worker months").

[147]Texts which seem to document an amount of grain in connection with ⊕, that is, grain which can be interpreted as feed, are seldom in the proto-elamite corpus. In *MDP* 17, 256, for example, ⊕ stands in a relation to grain of 2 ⊳ of grain per ⊕ (see the notation rev. ⧉ 3 • 2 ⊳ ⊕ 1 •). That would be, assuming a monthly ration, 2 ✳, or, according to our interpretation, ca. 1 1/2 liters per day. The same phenomenon is *not* evidenced by the text *MDP* 26S, 5011, since collation has shown that the first notation records the summation of grain measures disbursed to the small cattle ⹀; the second notation ⊕ 8 • ⌜4 ⊳⌝ will thus have also been a grain notation.

[148]Cf. R. Dittmann in U. Finkbeiner and W. Röllig, eds., *Ǧamdat Naṣr: Period or Regional Style?*, 332-366. A general idea of the numbers of animals documented archeologically in early Elamite settlements may be had from M. Zeder, "Understanding Urban Process through the Study of Specialized Subsistence Economy in the Near East," *Journal of Anthropological Archaeology* 7 (1988) 1-55 (in particular for the site Malyan). The very great preponderance of caprid bones in the Banesh assemblage at Malyan may help to explain the fact that we have been unable to posit any correspondence in the proto-elamite sign repertory to the proto-cuneiform signs AB_2 and GU_4 (large cattle).

names. All the names in a text may be introduced by this sign; for the most part, however, only the name in the first entry of a text is separated by the sign ⊳ from the heading of the text.[149] The interpretation of the sign ⊳ as a category of workers differs from other interpretations given in current literature[150] and therefore requires justification. Our interpretation is essentially based on three considerations:

1. The sign ⊳ is used in two clearly different functions. On the one hand it is used as a symbol qualifying names. On the other hand it is used as an ideogram for objects[151] together with numerical notations in the decimal system, which is commonly used in connection with counted animals. This double function of the sign ⊳ to serve as an ideogram for certain counted objects and at the same time to qualify names suggests that the sign denotes a category of workers or slaves, thus either qualifying a numerical notation or designating personal names as individuals belonging to this category.[152] This is strongly recommended also by the fact that in the proto-cuneiform texts ideograms for workers or slaves and ideograms for animals differ in that the latter are never connected with names, whereas texts about workers and even texts about "slaves" often include names with the registered persons. The interpretation that the sign in its first function associates a name with a special category of workers and in its second function denotes these workers themselves is especially obvious in texts with the sign in both functions at the same time.[153]

---

[149]Some of the names are occasionally qualified by the sign ⊳ others are not (for instance in MDP 26, 329) without any recognizably consistent rule of application. W. Brice, *Fs. E. Grumach*, p. 38, discusses the same inconsistency of signs designating other counted objects (Brice: "key signs") occasionally left implicit in the sources. It may be simply a matter of scribal choice which resulted in the inconsistent qualification of names with the sign ⊳ ; in TY 13, names of text TY 11 appear, however like most names in TY 13 without qualification by ⊳ .

[150]P. Meriggi, *Scrittura* I passim and *Acta Mycenaea* 2, 12, following V. Scheil (cp. *MDP* 17, p. 4 to no. 18; p. 6 to no. 45 and p. 18 to no. 120), relates the sign to the Sumerian sign TUR and assumes the meaning "small" or "son," whereas J. Friberg, *ERBM* I, 24-26, following W. Brice, *Bulletin of the John Rylands Library* 45, 15-39, seemingly tends to assume that it denotes an animal or is a determinative for animals in general. He differentiates however between this usage and the application of the sign in association with "bread and beer rations" in certain texts, in which case it should denote humans.

[151]Cf. the texts *MDP* 6, 399, 4997; *MDP* 17, 45; *MDP* 26, 52; *MDP* 26S, 5045.

[152]This double function cannot easily be explained under the assumption that the sign denotes the qualification "small" or an animal.

[153]The text *MDP* 17, 45, for instance, lists after a heading seven entries, each including a name/title and a numerical notation in the decimal system. The total of the seven entries on the reverse is qualified by the sign ⊳ . This makes clear that in all entries counted ⊳ are recorded, although only the first entry explicitly notes ⊳ as the quantified object. In the second, third and fourth entries the sign ⊳ seems to be substituted by the sign —, a horizontal stroke possibly with a similar function as in the texts TY 2 and 5. It can however not be excluded that the sign has a numerical function, since each entry in the first section of the text was qualified by 1 —, whereas a second section of the text contains a subheading qualified by 2 —. In the same text the sign ⊳ appears in the function of a sign qualifying names/titles. The sign precedes the name in the first entry and possibly also in the sixth entry, following a repetition of part of the global heading of the text. Even more suggestive is the use of the sign ⊳ in the two functions in the text *MDP* 6, 4997. According to our interpretation, which differs in substance from that of W. Brice, *Bulletin of the John Rylands Library* 45, 31-32, the text can be completely understood as an account of monthly (?) grain rations (sign ⊿) for workers of the category ⊳ with precisely the same size of rations as is attested for ⊳ in the texts *MDP* 6, 223, 236 (grain notation 1 ⊳ 2! — 1 ⊿, collated), 365 and *MDP* 26S, 4773 and 4803. The text records three hierarchical levels of workers, all of which can be designated as ⊳ . The highest level is represented by two named officials qualified as ⊳ . These two officials appear both on the obverse!, heading entries recording subordinate working groups together with their grain rations as well as on the reverse!, heading totals of workers (111 and 53 respectively) qualified as ⊳ and followed by notations representing the total grain disbursed to these workers. As can be clearly reconstructed from an analysis of the summations, the officials are not only qualified as ⊳ , but are themselves included in the sum of the ⊳ -workers. This proves that the sign ⊳ has the same meaning in both functions. In contrast

The number of objects designated by the sign ⯈ may be quite high in the texts from Susa—in one case 591, in another together with ≻ 1774+ of these objects are counted—so that the sign surely cannot denote a high-ranking official.[154]

2. The sign ⯈ in its function denoting quantified objects is often used parallel to signs which usually are interpreted as signs for persons.[155] We mention in particular the signs ≻, ⊲, *, ⯈, ⯈, ⯈, ⯈, ⨯⯈ and ⨯⯈.[156] There are several texts in the proto-elamite corpus with the signs ⯈ and ≻ which exhibit similarities to proto-cuneiform texts with the graphically similar signs KUR and SAL (⯇ and ▷).[157] These texts can be interpreted to be documents concerning the disbursement of rations to, or otherwise the organization and administrative dispensation of slaves or similar low-rank workers.

3. There are several texts with a fixed quantitative relation between the number of ⯈ and quantities of grain, so that the sign must denote an object which produces, consumes or is made of grain. Each ⯈ corresponds to 1/2 ⬭ grain.[158] The most reasonable interpretation seems to be that these texts record grain rations for ⯈.[159]

---

to the notations on the obverse, the two officials are further qualified on the reverse by a sign ◌ placed after their names, which may be a designation of their superior rank. The entries on the obverse of the tablet offer the exact hierarchical structure of the subordinated working groups. The first official is responsible for five, the second for three groups, each with a separately calculated grain notation. These groups with the exception of the last have the following structure: each consists of two sub-groups of ten persons under the supervision of one named overseer. The names of the overseers are, again, always qualified by the sign ⯈. The first official is thus responsible for five groups of 22 persons, that is, altogether 110 ⯈, each of whom received the same grain ration of 1/2 ⬭ noted below. The structure of the groups subordinate to the second official is precisely the same, except that the last group is incomplete, consisting of only one sub-group with eight workers and one overseer.

[154]See the texts MDP 17, 45 and MDP 26, 205 cited above, fn. 146. The proto-cuneiform sources record for the most part quite low numbers of SAL (▷) and KUR (⯇); one exception is the Uruk IV period text ATU 1, no. 577 with a notation on the reverse of 3 ⊳ ˈ3● 1 ◌ˈ [ ] SAL+KUR (collated), or "211+ female and male slaves/workers."

[155]See P. Meriggi, Acta Mycenaea 2, p. 14 and Scrittura I, 39-50. V. Scheil, MDP 17, p. 16 to no. 113, had already noted the graphic similarity between proto-elamite ≻ and proto-cuneiform ▷.

[156]See for example the texts MDP 6, 243, 246+332 (join confirmed in the Louvre, July 1988), 269, 324, 5006; MDP 17, 43, 120, 184, 292; MDP 26, 51. We interpret the sign ⦂ to be the sign corresponding to proto-cuneiform TUR (◌) and translate "child." According to this interpretation, the signs ⦂ and ⦂ may be compared with Sumerian dumu.SAL and dumu.nita and translated "male/female (slave?/worker?) child"; related signs inscribed in ⦂ should then denote the children of the given worker categories.

[157]The likely account text MDP 26, 205 records an imposing total of 1774+ ⯈≻, fully parallel to the convention in proto-cuneiform documents of qualifying a sum consisting of a mixed number of male (KUR) and female (SAL) "slaves"/"workers" with SAL+KUR. This qualification is in current literature (including ATU 2) often falsely transliterated géme, the later Sumerian designation for *female* slaves/workers alone.

[158]According to our interpretation of the absolute size of the proto-elamite ŠE-system units offered above, that would represent roughly 12 liters, corresponding to 1/2 month's rations for workers known from contemporary Mesopotamian sources. We have stated that since rations for just a half month would be unusual, the proto-elamite measures may have been approximately twice as large as those suspected for Mesopotamia of the same time.

[159]Our main text references for this interpretation are the texts MDP 6, 223, 236, 365 and MDP 26S, 4773 and 4803. In four of these cases the sign ⯈ is further qualified by ⤬. In the texts MDP 26, 156, 157, 160, 161, 171 and 220 and MDP 26S, 4771, on the other hand, the same rations are listed simply for ⤬ (counted also in the decimal system). We assume therefore that ⤬ is a further qualification of workers of the category ⯈. All five texts listing grain rations for ⯈ bear also a name qualified by ⯈ and may be documents of single transactions, whereas the texts with grain for ⤬ contain no such names and may represent accounts. The text MDP 26, 84 contains grain for ⤬ together with grain for ◌ (second sign on tablet, damaged), which is a pictogram of a plough parallel to the Sumerian sign APIN (APIN counted in the sexagesimal system). Texts with grain for ◌ are well attested in Susa, always with the same ratio of 2 ⚊ per ◌, which is four fifths of the grain for ⤬. We propose to interpret the grain for

The text Tepe Yahya 13

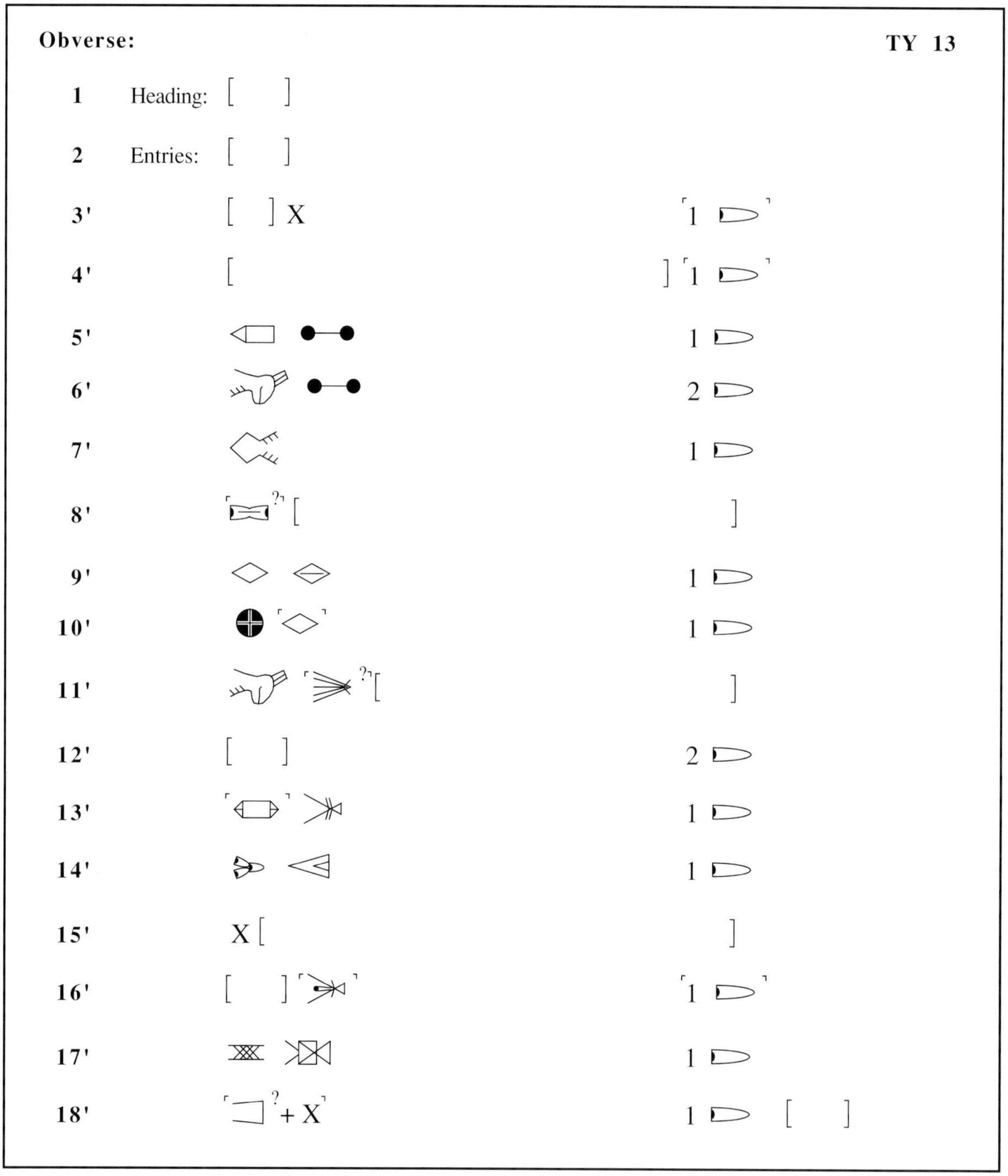

Obverse: TY 13

1	Heading: [ ]		
2	Entries: [ ]		
3'	[ ] X		⌐1 ▷¬
4'	[		] ⌐1 ▷¬
5'	◁☐ ●—●		1 ▷
6'	⬳ ●—●		2 ▷
7'	⬔		1 ▷
8'	⌐⋈¬⁈ [		]
9'	◇ ◈		1 ▷
10'	⊕ ⌐◇¬		1 ▷
11'	⬳ ⌐≫¬⁈[		]
12'	[ ]		2 ▷
13'	⌐◁☐▷¬ ✳		1 ▷
14'	⤳ ◁		1 ▷
15'	X [		]
16'	[ ]⌐✳¬		⌐1 ▷¬
17'	▦ ⧄		1 ▷
18'	⌐◹¬⁈+ X¬		1 ▷ [ ]

Figure 31. Transliteration of TY 13.

⬟ as rations for workers charged with plowing and seeding one unit of ◁ ; ◁ itself remains unclear, but may be connected with a known unit of work or even field measure. *MDP* 26, 117 and 174 with notations including △ = "1/2" ◁ make the usual translation "plow" of this sign suspect, as we have stated above, fn. 115. Furthermore, since ◁ are counted sexagesimally and not, as for ▷ and ⬟, decimally, it follows that ◁ cannot denote the workers involved in plowing. If we may assume first that ◁ is a measure of an area which was to be sown with 2 —, second that the absolute size of the proto-elamite grain units of the ŠE system are not the same as but rather approximately *twice* as large as in proto-cuneiform texts (cf. the discussion above of the ŠE system), then 1 ◁ in Susa would very closely correspond to 1 IKU in Mesopotamia.

The text TY 13 is a fragment of a large text with several entries. Unfortunately, the heading is broken away and no entry contains a sign expressing the nature of the counted objects. The entries consist of names followed by numerical notations, each of which is either 1 ⊂▷ or 2 ⊂▷. It is likely that these notations represent always one or two discrete objects.

That the ideographic sign combinations at the beginning of each entry represent names is evident not only from the text format. Four, possibly five of the ideographic sign combinations of this text correspond to names attested in the text TY 11: ⟨⟨, ◇ ⬦, ⤳ ≫, ⊂▷ ⤜ and [◁] ⤜?. Both texts thus obviously derive from the same context; it seems likely that in text TY 13 sheep were also registered. The entries differ, however, from the entries of the text TY 11 not only by the absence of ideograms representing quantified objects but also by the fact that with one exception no personal name is introduced by the sign ⧽.

The rationing text Tepe Yahya 12

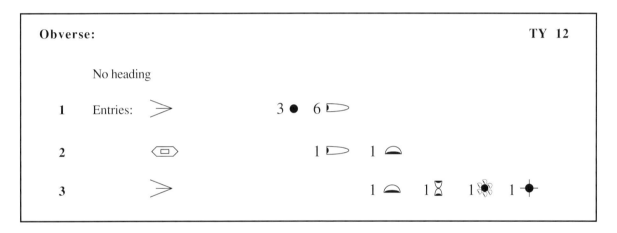

Figure 32. Transliteration of TY 12.

The Text TY 12 is a small, well preserved text without a heading and without identification of institutions or persons. Only two logograms, ⟩ and ⊂▢▷, indicate quantified objects. Nevertheless, the text is one of the most interesting texts of the Tepe Yahya corpus, since it might belong to a relatively small group of proto-elamite texts exhibiting a strict numerical relation between two different objects.

Since it was associated with a numerical notation including 6 ⊂▷, the sign ⟩ represented an object which was quantified with a system used for discrete units, probably with the decimal system.[160] The numerical notation following the first entry therefore represents 36 units of ⟩. The sign ⊂▢▷ is usually used with the ŠE system, although it may also be used with a system for discrete counting, probably the bisexagesimal system.[161] In the present

---

[160]See *MDP* 26, 205 and our comments on the sign combination ⟩ ▷ in fns. 76, 146 and 149.

[161]This corresponds to the use of the proto-cuneiform sign GAR ("NINDA"), for which see *ATU* 2, p. 133 and 141. The assumption that the sign ⊂▷ can be used with the bisexagesimal system is primarily derived from the fact that it is very often used as a collective logogram for different grain products which are clearly counted with the bisexagesi-

case, the sign ⌒ makes clear that the numerical notation following the sign ⟨▭⟩ is a notation in the ŠE system. Hence the entry represents 6 ⌒ or 36 ✳. This correspondence between 1 ⟩ and 1 ✳ may of course be fortuitous, but it is more likely that it results from a correspondence between the number of ⟩ and the units of ⟨▭⟩.

According to our interpretation, ⟩ corresponds to the proto-cuneiform sign SAL denoting a female slave or low-ranking worker.[162] P. Meriggi has convincingly argued that the sign ⟨⫿⟩ and its variants such as ⟨▭⟩ correspond to the proto-cuneiform sign GAR/NINDA and therefore probably represent (bread/grain?-)rations.[163] The first two entries can therefore be interpreted as registering (bread/grain?-)rations for female workers apportioned in a grain capacity measure. The size of the measures imply that the text dealt with daily rations.[164]

The meaning of the last entry is far less clear. It consists again of the sign ⟩ followed by a numerical notation, however in this case a notation in the ŠE system, thus representing not a number of female workers but rather an amount of grain. If we assume that this grain is again composed of rations of the size ✳ it would be the amount disbursed to 10 workers (or for ten workdays performed by an indeterminate number of female workers) with an unclear addition of 5% represented by the sign ✦. This may be an "administrative adjustment," although its nature is completely unclear.

Unclear applications

Both texts *Tepe Yahya 26* and *27* are in a state of preservation which precludes their assignment to one of the above discussed text categories. If however the tentative reconstruction of the text TY 27 is correct, this text may have recorded amounts of grain.

---

mal system. A proto-elamite example for the use of a variant of ⟨▭⟩ with a system for counted discrete objects can be found on the fragment *MDP* 6, 222. This fragment belonged to a text with a structure very similar to the text *MDP* 6, 4997 discussed in fn. 153. Instead of the grain rations ⌑, however, the fragment lists (bread/grain?-)rations ⟨▭⟩ for a hierarchically structured group of ⟩.

[162]See fns. 76 and 146-149.

[163]*Scrittura* I, 73-78.

[164]This conclusion can be drawn first from the size of the small units of the ŠE-System which served either without further qualification, or as signs inscribed in such logograms as ⌐, to denote grain rations. They range for the most part from a quantity represented by ⌇ up to ⌑. Because they are the smallest units attested in the ŠE system, they will probably have represented complete or partial daily rations. Second, the size of the rations in TY 12 may be compared to rations in similar texts. The text *MDP* 26, 125 has on its reverse a total 3 ⌒ 1 ⌇ 1 ✳ qualified as ⟨▭⟩. This total results from entries 4 X (sign damaged in copy) and 20 ⌐ × ✳. The sign X thus represents an amount of grain corresponding to the unit ✳. Each of the 20 units subsumed under ⟨▭⟩ represents the amount ✳, exactly as in the text TY 12. On the other hand, several texts document grain rations for workers qualified as ⩘ or ⩘ ⟩ (see fn. 146) of 2 1/2 ⌒, which in *MDP* 26S, 4771 are explicitly subsumed under a total qualified as ⟨▭⟩. These rations are exactly 15 times higher than the assumed daily rations for ⟩. We believe therefore that they are monthly rations half as large as would have been the case in the present text. The text *MDP* 6, 399 however does not fit into this scheme. Entries about variously qualified workers of the category ⟩, including workers of the category ⩘ ⟩, add up to the 1412 ⟩ registered in the total. This total of workers is followed by a grain notation qualified as ⟨▭⟩ corresponding to 1412 ⌒, i.e., two fifths of the amount usually attested for ⩘ ⟩ and interpreted here as monthly rations. Third, according to our estimation of the absolute sizes of the proto-elamite ŠE system (see our discussion of the ŠE system above), a ration of ✳ may have corresponded to a quantity of approximately 0.7 l. Data from proto-cuneiform texts suggest that this is the daily ration of an adult laborer.

```
┌────────────────────────────────────────────────────────────────────┐
│  Obverse:                                                     TY  26 │
│                                                                      │
│    1     Heading:      [     ]                                       │
│                                                                      │
│    2'    Entries:     [                    ] ⌐4▭¬                    │
│                                                                      │
└────────────────────────────────────────────────────────────────────┘
```

```
┌────────────────────────────────────────────────────────────────────┐
│  Obverse:                                                     TY  27 │
│                                                                      │
│    1     Heading:      [     ]                                       │
│                                                                      │
│    2'    Entries:    ⌐▱×?¬ [              ] ⌐2?▭¬                    │
│                                                                      │
└────────────────────────────────────────────────────────────────────┘
```

Figure 33. Transliterations of TY 26-27.

THE TEPE YAHYA TEXTS IN THE PROTO-ELAMITE SETTING

The corpus of proto-elamite texts from Tepe Yahya presented in this volume is clearly too small to allow of definitive statements about the script in use in this small settlement or about the nature of the administrative unit which resulted in the production and possible storage of these documents. Still, it will be important here to attempt a comparison and contrast between the texts from Yahya and those from other proto-elamite sites and to review the historical and administrative developments in Susiana and the Iranian plateau in general, in Yahya in particular, to which our texts can serve as witness. Such comparisons may be based not only on analyses of contextual sign usages, but also on the structure and format of administrative documents.

Certain features particularly of tablet format shared between texts from different sites may be interpreted, for instance, to indicate the administrative dependence of one site on another, probably larger site. Tablet collections from Tepe Yahya and Tal-e Malyan (ancient Anshan) exhibit in some measure such common administrative formats, ideograms and titles. A very good example from both settlements is the use of the sign ▷, which we have interpreted to designate a male slave or low-ranking worker. Exact parallels to the Yahya text TY 11, which deals with numbers of animals probably in the charge of persons called ▷, could be cited from Susa. Furthermore, signs such as ▷ and ▨, according to their position in the tablet formats to be considered headings probably indicating administrative units, belong to the most common signs in the collections from Susa, Malyan and Yahya.[165]

---

[165]Only three signs from the Malyan tablets known to us may be used in a comparison between the writing systems of Malyan and Susa and those of Malyan and Yahya, respectively. The signs ▷ and ▷ are common to Malyan (▷: M-626 [unpubl., courtesy M. Stolper], M-632 in M. Stolper, *Kadmos* 24, 6, M-1000 in W. Sumner, *Iran* 14, pl. IIIh; ▷: M-1155 in M. Stolper, *Kadmos* 24, 7 [photo obv. I. Nicholas, *Expedition* 23/3, 45 and W. Sumner, *Iran* 14, pl.

Our experience with proto-elamite texts from Yahya and other sites, in particular from Malyan, leads us however to caution against an ascription of such shared features in the "provincial"[166] documents exclusively or even primarily to willful colonial activity; the similarity of the proto-elamite texts from these outlying sites to those from Susa seems, in fact, less suggestive of political or economic control of these settlements by interests centered in or around Susa—or for that matter any other external center—than of the mundane functioning of more or less independent economic units. The discovery of 84 "tablet blanks" together with the inscribed Yahya tablets in the same building complex may not be sufficient evidence to dismiss the contention that the tablets might themselves have been brought into Yahya, since we are not entirely convinced that these clay objects were uninscribed tablets.[167] The texts, so far as we have been able to classify them, record however the dispensation of products from agricultural activity, in particular the rationing of quantities of grain to presumable workers under the direction of household administrators, and possibly the disbursement of grain for the purpose of sowing, as we think, rather unimposing fields.[168] The level of these administrative notations, the size of the recorded numbers of animals and humans and the measures of grain, are without exception entirely within the range of expected *local* activity.

The level of this activity is thus only to be distinguished from other periods in Yahya and elsewhere by the fact that it was, during the proto-elamite period, documented by "proto-elamite" administrators. The documentation was in fact short-lived; as C. Lamberg-Karlovsky has argued, the entire proto-elamite occupation might have lasted no more than 100 years and in that time cultural remains—including the tablets—were deposited in a single building complex.[169] This situation as well as the fact that there was no archeological evidence in Yahya suggesting that this apparent foreign element had assumed administrative control of the settlement by force[170] might be indicative of a peaceful coexistence between an indigenous population and administrators of foreign origin; whether they were only inspired by or were in direct contact and exchange with an external political center cannot, given the present state of

---

IIId; //M-1156, unpubl., courtesy M. Stolper]) and Susa, against both [sign] and [sign] and [sign] in Yahya; the Yahya sign [sign], in particular, might represent an administrative unit dependent on the units designated [sign] in Malyan and Susa. Malyan (M-1476 and 1477 [unpubl., courtesy M. Stolper]) and Yahya share, on the other hand, the use of the numerical sign form [sign] against [sign] in Susa (see the comparison of the proto-elamite and the proto-cuneiform numerical systems above).

[166]We use "provincial" with some circumspection, since one of the "provincial" sites, Malyan, may have been several times larger than Susa in the proto-elamite period. Cf. the discussion below, fn. 171.

[167]Cf. C. Lamberg-Karlovsky, *Kadmos* 10, 98-99 and the photograph at the end of this volume. The "tablet blanks" were found in the same room and with approximately the same length and width, in most cases however clearly not the same thickness, as TY 1-6. Comparable clay objects were also found in Uruk period Godin Tepe (cf. H. Weiss and T. Young, *Iran* 13, 10, to tablet no. 2) and Tepe Hissar (cf. fn. 8 above).

[168]Cf. below to the numerical GAN$_2$ system and see C. Lamberg-Karlovsky, *Antiquity* 52, 117-118.

[169]We refer for a presentation of the find situation to Lamberg-Karlovsky's treatment of tablet excavations in the introduction to this volume (see also id., "Foreign Relations in the Third Millennium at Tepe Yahya," in *Le plateau iranien et l'Asie centrale des origines à la conquête islamique* [=*Actes du Colloque international du CNRS* no. 567; Paris 1977] 33-43).

[170]R. Girshman's suggestion in *Fouilles de Sialk* I, 58 that the proto-elamite phase may have been ushered in there by destructive force has been undermined by P. Amiet, *L'âge* 68, who demonstrates in Sialk's material remains a likely "peaceful" coexistence between proto-elamite and indigenous populations. Girshman's ash layer itself, moreover, apparently covered only a restricted area of the mound.

insufficient documentation, be determined.[171]

In light of our currently still very limited understanding of proto-elamite ideography, much information will doubtless be lost about the economic activities recorded in the "provincial" as in the Susa texts due simply to the fact that we do not understand the meaning of sign combinations which according to tablet format in all likelihood represent professional titles or personal names. One might, for example, hope to find in such designations references to stone cutters, to smiths, even to trade agents. The complete absence of references in these texts to the exploited resources of the regions, in particular to metals and stone, suggest that such exploitation, if at all recorded, will have been secondary to primary agricultural activities in the respective settlements. In the case of Tepe Yahya, it seems that such intensive exploitation of raw materials, particularly chlorite,[172] set in substantially after the close of the proto-elamite "incursion" there.

Proto-elamite texts themselves offer as yet no clear testimony in this debate. Reservations felt about the current value of such historical testimony are understandable in light of the very limited interpretive possibilities research in archaic documents has presented to date, compared with the wealth of information to be found in excavation reports and with the theoretical models derived from archeological and ethnological data. Yet the importance of historical questions surrounding the period of urbanization in which archaic texts appeared in Western Asia is certainly very great and the organizational pressures from emerging new societies which make the development and daily use of writing understandable should be of imposing interest to historians and ethnologists alike. Material remains and to a substantially lesser extent early texts inform us that such societies, which may themselves be termed "archaic," operated at a

---

[171]J. Alden inspired in *Current Anthropology* 23/6, 613-628, a provocative discussion of such involved developments; cf. the comments by leading specialists in the field, reply and extensive bibliography pp. 629-640. In this regard, we wish only to underscore two points made op.cit. by P. Kohl and H. Nissen. Alden's thesis of a proto-elamite hegemony in the proto-elamite/Jemdet Nasr period (3050 - 2900 B.C., corresponding to "Late Middle Banesh") centered not in Susa but rather in Malyan is based on a very tenuous archeological record and collides with the evidence known from texts unearthed at both sites. Published (cf. fn. 7 above) and unpublished (courtesy of M. Stolper) tablets from Malyan/Anshan are indicative of economic activities greater than those of Tepe Yahya, yet by no means in the order of the larger Susa accounts. Contrary to the comments of C. Lamberg-Karlovsky (based on P. Meriggi) in *Current Anthropology* 23/6, p. 632, the texts from Susa record very large numbers of animals as well as notations of grain measures as large as the largest such notations known from proto-cuneiform texts. Cp. the texts *MDP* 17, 275-276 (collated) with a minimum count of 1502 and 901 head of small cattle respectively, *MDP* 31, 31, rev., with 23,600ˢⁱᶜ of the animals •◄ (collated) and *MDP* 26, 48 with notations corresponding to a minimum of 17,100 of the grain measures ▷ (*MDP* 26, 362, with approximately 4 times as much grain, is a school text, for which see above, fns. 51-53. The *largest* but possibly atypical cereal notation in the proto-cuneiform corpus [W19726,a; published in *ATU* 2, pl. 58 and P. Damerow, R. Englund and H. Nissen, *Spektrum der Wissenschaft*, March 1988, p. 47] represents ca. 36,000 of the grain measures ▷; the *second* largest corresponds to 5400 ▷ [W22123,c; unpublished]). We are not competent to judge the archeological merits of the various centers which might have played a major role in the proto-elamite expansion into Tepe Yahya, namely Susa (implied by C. Lamberg-Karlovsky, *Antiquity* 52, 118 and elsewhere), Malyan (cf. J. Alden, *Current Anthropology* 23, 621) or an as yet unexcavated site in the vicinity of Yahya. T. Beale mentioned in his survey report, "Tepe Yahya Project: Soghun Valley Survey," *Iran* 14 (1976) 174-175, a site less than 1 km from Yahya measuring 10 hectares in the Yahya periods VB, IVC and IVB, that is a site substantially larger than Yahya; R. Dittmann, *BBVO* 4/1, 483-487, considered this site a possible candidate for the center responsible for or even directing activities in Yahya. For a good general introduction to the cultural context of Tepe Yahya in the archaic period see D. Potts, *The Late 4th Millennium Universe of a Highland Community in Iran* (Ann Arbor 1977), and for an involved discussion of the settlement patterns in the region surrounding Yahya M. Prickett, *Man, Land and Water: Settlement Distribution and the Development of Irrigation Agriculture in the Upper Rud-i Gushk Drainage, Southeastern-Iran*, vol. 2 (Ann Arbor 1986) 782-786.

[172]See C. Lamberg-Karlovsky, *Urban Interaction on the Iranian Plateau: Excavations at Tepe Yahya 1967-1973*, (Oxford 1974) 36-39.

stage well removed from that of so-called primitive cultures. The mere fact of a centralized administration, be it local or regional, as well as the quantities of the goods and workers registered in archaic texts document, in our opinion, an at least inchoate form of class division into a functioning administrative elite and laborers, probably with a concomitant shift of ownership of in particular productive land to a small group within the community. This more advanced organization replaced tribal or simply familial organization in village settings. It has in large part been the subject of archeological conjecture to interpret the data found together with clay tablets in the proto-elamite settlements of ancient Persia which throw light on these early developments. We believe that further analysis of the proto-elamite tablets offers growing hope of establishing controls of archeological hypotheses, if not in due time of themselves serving as documents with direct testimony to the events in proto-literate Western Asia.

SIGNLIST

The following signlist is divided into two sections, comprised of the "ideograms" (a term used conventionally to designate those signs which may have had ideographic, logographic or possibly syllabic function) and the numerical signs in the Yahya corpus. The first section is ordered according to the signlist compiled by R. de Mecquenem in *MDP* 31; in some cases, one of a number of signform candidates from *MDP* 31 was chosen which seemed graphically closest to the Yahya sign. As far as possible, we have made reference to signs in that signlist, even in the cases of signforms which are not identical. In such cases, an asterisk following the sign number in *MDP* 31 implies that the Yahya form is a close parallel and may represent a redundant variation. Those Yahya signs for which we were able to find no Susa parallels or which seem to be non-redundant variants are included at the end of the list with the reference "Not in *MDP* 31". Following the individual signlist references are to be found first the text references of the respective signs in the Yahya corpus, second where applicable those texts in which the sign in question may be the designation of an object, and third comments about the function or graphical peculiarities of the sign. The second section of the signlist, the numerical signs, is ordered according to the section of the Uruk signlist *ATU* 2 devoted to proto-cuneiform numerical signs. Those signs having forms not attested in *ATU* 2 are registered with a following qualification "var" (=variant).

Ideographic signs

—	*MDP* 31:	2
	References:	TY 2, 5, 14 and 25
	Comment:	Dividing line in TY 2 and 5?
⊏⊐	*MDP* 31:	5[?]
	Reference:	TY 2
	Object:	TY 2 (first entry beginning with: ⊏⊐ ◇ ⋈, total: ⊏⊐ ◇).
	Comment:	No justification for the signform in the lapidary texts B, H2 and K, cited *MDP* 31, p. 45 to sign no. 5.
⟋	*MDP* 31:	40
	Reference:	TY 14
⟍	*MDP* 31:	100
	Reference:	TY 11

	MDP 31:	198
	Reference:	TY 11

	MDP 31:	282-285
	Reference:	TY 11

	MDP 31:	388
	Reference:	TY 14
	Comment:	◁ in *MDP* 31 drawn too large; cp. the reference text *MDP* 17, 425 and the sign *MDP* 31, 2267.

	MDP 31:	602
	Reference:	TY 11

	MDP 31:	653*
	Reference:	TY 24
	Comment:	Middle circle incised.

	MDP 31:	662-664
	Reference:	TY 16
	Comment:	The use of the numerical sign ● as part of the Susa sign must be determined by inspecting tablet original or photo.

	MDP 31:	721
	References:	TY 15 and 18
	Object:	TY 15? (═ ⊐□)

	MDP 31:	749
	Reference:	TY 3
	Object:	TY 3
	Comment:	The sign may be a variant of ≋.

	MDP 31:	780
	Reference:	TY 13

	MDP 31:	845
	Reference:	TY 11?

	MDP 31:	1219-1230
	References:	TY 15, 18, 21, 23 and 25
	Object:	TY 15? (═══ ⊐), TY 18 (total: ⊐), TY 21 (⊐ ◇), TY 23 and 25?

	MDP 31:	1219*
	Reference:	TY 14
	Comment:	Compositum not attested in Susa.

	MDP 31:	1474
	Reference:	TY 11
	Comment:	Cp. *MDP* 31, 1697* (⬛) and the sign ⬛ below.

	MDP 31:	1697*
	Reference:	TY 17
	Comment:	Difference between *MDP* 31, 1697 and 1697*: oblique bars are discontinuous; cp. *MDP* 31, 110, 1474 (⬛), and the sign ⬛ below.

	MDP 31:	1761*
	Reference:	TY 14
	Comment:	Difference between *MDP* 31, 1761 and 1761*: 4 instead of 3 bars on either side of rectangle.

	MDP 31:	Cp. 1836ff.
	Reference:	TY 19

	MDP 31:	1849*
	Reference:	TY 11
	Comment:	Difference between *MDP* 31, 1849 and 1849*: Inscribed sign possibly a compositum of a doubled *MDP* 31, 2321.

	MDP 31:	1877
	References:	TY 7 and 14
	Comment:	Form with quadrilobe attested in Yahya, Susa and Malyan.

	MDP 31:	1877*
	References:	TY 1, 3, 4 and 23
	Comment:	Difference between *MDP* 31, 1877 and 1877*: Inscribed sign tri- instead of quadrilobe. Sign attested only in Yahya.

	MDP 31:	1914-1915
	Reference:	TY 11

	MDP 31:	1941-1942
	Reference:	TY 18

	MDP 31:	2150-2151
	References:	TY 1, 2, 5, 19 and 20
	Object:	TY 1 (≋, ≋ ▰, ◇, ≋ ⫸, total: ≋ ⬰), TY 2, 5, 19 (≋ ⬰), TY 20

	MDP 31:	2192-2194
	Reference:	TY 14

	MDP 31:	2225-2226, 2228-2232
	References:	TY 11, 12, 14 and 18
	Object:	TY 12, 14?, 18?

	MDP 31:	2321
	Reference:	TY 1
	Object:	TY 1 (≋ 〉〉〉〉〉〉—)
	Comment:	Cp. the signs *MDP* 31, 129-134.

	MDP 31:	2483
	References:	TY 11 and 13

	MDP 31:	2524*
	References:	TY 11 and 13
	Comment:	Difference between *MDP* 31, 2524 and 2524*: the two vertical bars are oblique, cp. *MDP* 31, 2285.

	MDP 31:	2553-2560
	Reference:	TY 13

	MDP 31:	2632*, 2639*, 2641-2643*, 2648*, 2653*
	Reference:	TY 11
	Comment:	Difference between the Yahya and Susa forms: the vertical bar in 2632 is curved in the Yahya text. Cp. however the sign in the Susa text *MDP* 6, 353.

	MDP 31:	2693*
	Reference:	TY 18
	Comment:	Difference between *MDP* 31, 2693 and 2693*: asymmetrical sign, cp. the sign *MDP* 31, 5281.

	MDP 31:	2711 + ❋ ("N$_{30c}$"; see Numerical signlist below)
	Reference:	TY 8
	Object:	TY 8
	Comment:	Cp. the sign *MDP* 31, 2893.

	MDP 31:	2835
	Reference:	TY 11

	MDP 31:	3055*
	Reference:	TY 13
	Comment:	Difference between *MDP* 31, 3055 and 3055*: No inscribed ═══ (=*MDP* 31, 721).
	MDP 31:	3055**
	Reference:	TY 11
	Comment:	Difference between *MDP* 31, 3055 and 3055**: Inscribed sign ◇ (=*MDP* 31, 3662) instead of ═══.
	MDP 31:	3163
	Reference:	TY 13
	MDP 31:	3414
	Reference:	TY 11
	MDP 31:	3457-3461
	References:	TY 12, 14 and 17
	Object:	TY 12
	MDP 31:	3486-3490
	Reference:	TY 14
	MDP 31:	3520-3523
	References:	TY 11 and 13
	MDP 31:	3550-3551
	Reference:	TY 14
	MDP 31:	3661-3662
	References:	TY 11 and 13
	Comment:	Cp. the sign *MDP* 31, 3831.

	MDP 31:	3700, 3702, 3704, 3707
	References:	TY 1, 2, 3, 7, 11, 13 and 21
	Object:	TY 1, 2 (⬡ ⬦ ✗, —, total: ⬡ ⬦), TY 3, 7 and 21? (▷▢ ⬦)

	MDP 31:	3786
	Reference:	TY 6

	MDP 31:	4089-4093
	Reference:	TY 11

	MDP 31:	4164
	Reference:	TY 22

	MDP 31:	4314*
	References:	TY 6 and 22
	Comment:	Difference between *MDP* 31, 4314 and 4314*: extended ends on either side of sign.

	MDP 31:	4319-4330
	References:	TY 11, 14 and 24

	MDP 31:	4463 (with numerous variants)
	References:	TY 1, 2, 3, 4, 5, 19 and 27
	Object:	TY 1 (✗, not? included in total: ≋ ✗), TY 2 (qualifier in ⬡ ⬦ ✗), TY 3 (parallel to ≡ [=? ≋] and ⬦), TY 4, 5 (≋ ✗), TY 19 (obv.: ✗, rev.: ≋ ✗)

	MDP 31:	4785
	Reference:	TY 11
	Object:	TY 11 (repeated sequence: ⟫ PN? ✤, decimal numerical notation)

⊕	*MDP* 31:	5012-5013
	Reference:	TY 13
	Comment:	Signform is the sign ● with an incised cross.

●—●	*MDP* 31:	5120
	References:	TY 11 and 13

⋈	*MDP* 31:	5176
	References:	TY 6 and 11
	Comment:	Ideographic use of numerical sign? Cp. the sign *MDP* 31, 5305, which is considered the numerical variant of the ideogram *MDP* 31, 5176.

⋈	*MDP* 31:	5177
	References:	TY 13 and 14
	Comment:	Cp. the sign *MDP* 31, 5306 and see comment to the preceding sign in the present list.

⋈	*MDP* 31:	5184
	Reference:	TY 14
	Comment:	Cp. the signs *MDP* 31, 5312-5313 and see comment to the sign *MDP* 31, 5176 in the present list.

●≪	*MDP* 31:	5192
	Reference:	TY 8
	Object:	TY 8

●≋	*MDP* 31:	5206
	Reference:	TY 1
	Object:	TY 1 (qualification of ≋ ?)
	Comment:	Cp. the texts *MDP* 17, 64 and *MDP* 26, 201.

MDP 31:	5358*	
Reference:	TY 11	
Object:	TY 11 (repeated sequence: ⬭ PN? ⊕, decimal numerical notation)	
Comment:	Difference between *MDP* 31, 5358 and 5358*: the first two impressed ▷'s are oblique rather than parallel (⬭ instead of ▷). Sign only in Yahya.	

Not in *MDP* 31.	
Reference:	TY 14

Not in *MDP* 31.	
References:	TY 11 and 13?
Comment:	Signform *MDP* 31, 2256 with 3 long strokes and unclear bars on the right side.

Not in *MDP* 31.	
Reference:	TY 17
Object:	TY 17
Comment:	Cp. the signs *MDP* 31, 1474 (▨▨▨), 1697* and 2091-2139.

Not in *MDP* 31.	
Reference:	TY 17
Comment:	Signform uncertain. Cp. the signs *MDP* 31, 550-551 without impression of the butt end of the stylus.

Not in *MDP* 31.	
Reference:	TY 14
Comment:	Cp. the signs *MDP* 31, 4279-4302.

Not in *MDP* 31.	
Reference:	TY 11

	Not in *MDP* 31.	
	References:	TY 11 and 13

	Not in *MDP* 31.	
	Reference:	TY 11

	Not in *MDP* 31.	
	Reference:	TY 18

	Not in *MDP* 31.	
	Reference:	TY 18
	Comment:	Signform a doubled sign *MDP* 31, 5301? Cp. the signs *MDP* 31, 942, 1263 and 2264.

Numerical signs

	ATU 2:	N_1
	References:	passim

	ATU 2:	$N_1{}^{var}$
	References:	TY 1, 3, 7 and 21

	ATU 2:	N_{14}
	References:	TY 1, 2, 7, 11, 12, 16, 19, 21 and 23

	ATU 2:	$N_{14}{}^{var}$
	References:	TY 1, 2, 4, 6, 12, 14, 17, 21 and 22

⊡	*ATU* 2:	N$_{14}$^{var}
	References:	TY 7, 21 and 23
⧖	*ATU* 2:	N$_{24}$
	References:	TY 1, 2, 4, 5, 12, 14, 18, 20 and 21
⧖	*ATU* 2:	N$_{24}$^{var}
	References:	TY 1 and 14
✷	*ATU* 2:	N$_{30c}$
	References:	TY 1, 2, 4, 6, 12, 14, 17, 18, 20, 21 and 22
✷	*ATU* 2:	N$_{30}$^{var}
	References:	TY 1, 14 and 20
⌒	*ATU* 2:	N$_{39b}$
	References:	TY 1, 2, 3, 5, 7, 12, 18, 21 and 23
⌒	*ATU* 2:	N$_{39b}$^{var}
	References:	TY 14 and 20
	Comment:	Cp. the signs *MDP* 31, 4825-4826, and the texts *MDP* 26, 169 and 372.
⌒	*ATU* 2:	N$_{39b}$^{var}
	References:	TY 1 and 7
⌒	*ATU* 2:	N$_{43}$
	Reference:	TY 17
●	*ATU* 2:	N$_{45}$
	Reference:	TY 10

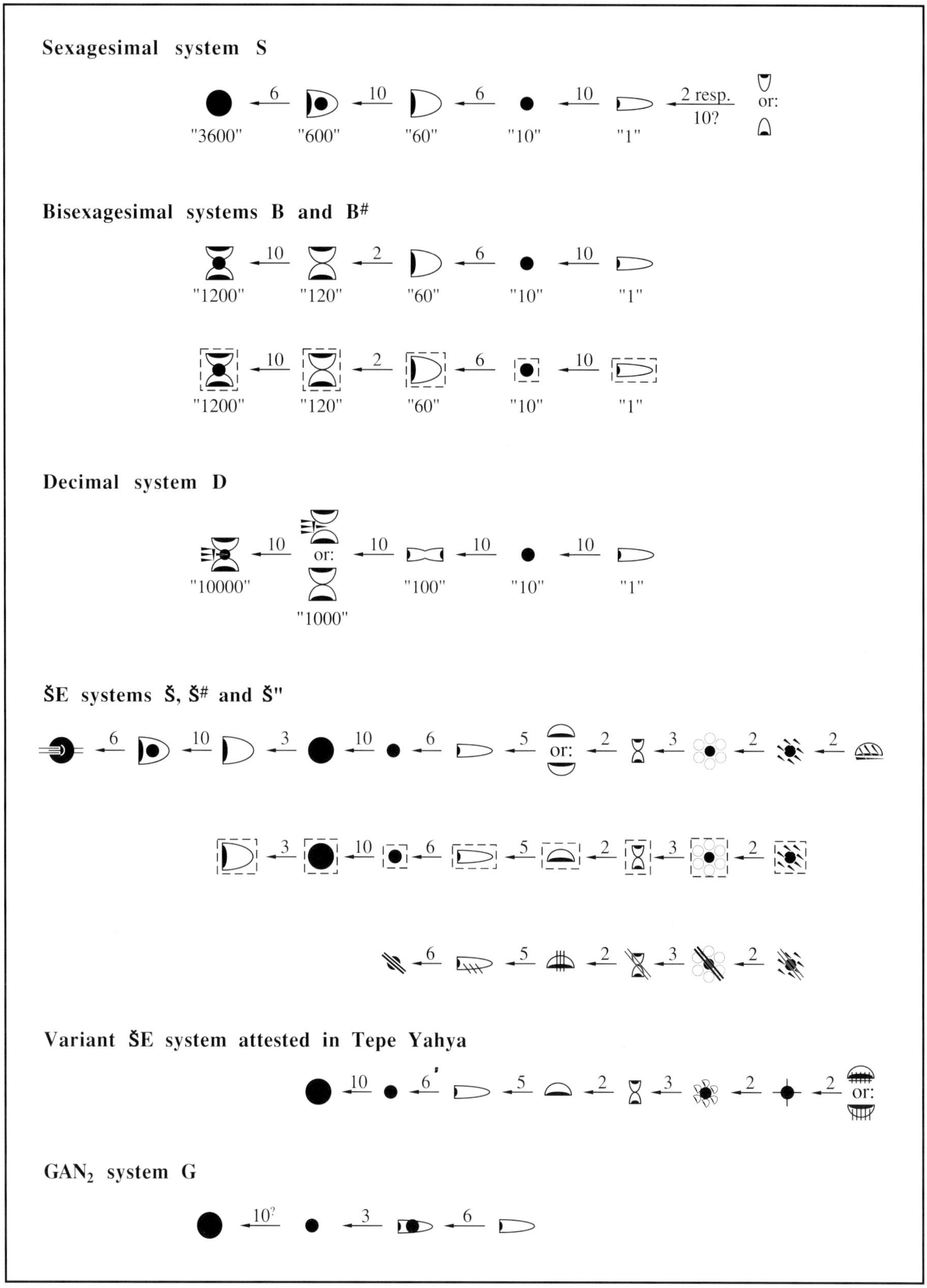

Sexagesimal system S

Bisexagesimal systems B and B#

Decimal system D

ŠE systems Š, Š# and Š"

Variant ŠE system attested in Tepe Yahya

GAN₂ system G

Figure 34. The proto-elamite numerical sign systems.

BIBLIOGRAPHY

Alden, J."Trade and Politics in Proto-Elamite Iran." *Current Anthropology* 23/6 (December 1982) 613-640.

Amiet, P. "Il y a 5000 ans: Les Elamites inventaient l'écriture." *Archaeologia* 12 (1966) 16-23.
_____. *Elam.* Anvers-sur-Oise 1966.
_____. *Glyptique susienne, des origines à l'époque des Perses Achéménides* (=*MDP* 43). Paris 1972.
_____. "La période IV de Tépé Sialk reconsidérée," in J.-L. Huot et al., eds., *De l'Indus aux Balkans* (=*Fs. Deshayes*). Paris 1985, 293-312
_____. *L'âge des échanges inter-iraniens.* Paris 1986.

Amiet, P., and Tosi, M. "Phase 10 at Shahr-i Sokhta." *East and West* 28 (1978) 9-31.

Beale, T. "Bevelled Rim Bowls and their Implications for Change and Economic Organization in the Later Fourth Millennium B.C." *JNES* 37 (1978) 289-313.

Brice, W. "The Writing System of the Proto-elamite Account Tablets of Susa." *Bulletin of the John Rylands Library* 45 (1962-1963) 15-39.
_____. "A Comparison of the Account Tablets of Susa in the Proto-elamite Script with those of Hagia Triada in Linear A." *Kadmos* 2 (1963) 27-38.
_____. "The Structure of Linear A, with some Proto-Elamite and Proto-Indic Comparisons," in W. Brice, ed., *Europa: Studien zur Geschichte und Epigraphik der frühen Aegaeis* (=*Fs. E. Grumach*). Berlin 1967, 32-44.

Bulgarelli, G. "The Lithic Industry of Tepe Hissar at the Light of Recent Excavation," in M. Taddei, ed., *South Asian Archaeology* 1977. Naples 1979, 39-54.

Carter, E., and Stolper, M. *Elam: Surveys of Political History and Archaeology.* Berkeley 1984.

Damerow, P. "Die Entstehung des arithmetischen Denkens," in P. Damerow and W. Lefèvre, eds., *Rechenstein, Experiment, Sprache.* Stuttgart 1981, 11-113.
_____. "Individual Development and Historical Evolution of Arithmetical Thinking," in S. Strauss, ed., *Ontogeny, Phylogeny and Historical Development* . Norwood, New Jersey, 1988.

Damerow, P., and Englund, R. "Die Zahlzeichensysteme der Archaischen Texte aus Uruk," in M. Green and H. Nissen, *Zeichenliste der Archaischen Texte aus Uruk* (=*ATU* 2). Berlin 1987, 117-166 + tables 54-60.

Damerow, P., Englund, R., and Nissen, H. "Zur rechnergestützten Bearbeitung der archaischen Texte aus Mesopotamien." *MDOG* 121 (1989; in press).

Dittmann, R. "Susa in the Proto-Elamite Period and Annotations on the Painted Pottery of Proto-Elamite Khuzestan," in U. Finkbeiner and W. Röllig, eds., *Ğamdat Naṣr: Period or Regional Style?* Wiesbaden 1986, 171-198.
_____. "Seals, Sealings and Tablets," in U. Finkbeiner and W. Röllig, eds., *Ğamdat Naṣr: Period or Regional Style?* Wiesbaden 1986, 332-366.
_____. *Betrachtungen zur Frühzeit des Südwest-Iran* (=*BBVO* 4). Berlin 1986.

Dyson, R. "The Relative and Absolute Chronology of Hissar II and the Proto-Elamite Horizon of Northern Iran," in O. Aurenche et al., eds., *Chronologies du Proche Orient* (= *BAR International Series* 379). Oxford 1987, 647-678

Englund, R. "Administrative Timekeeping in Ancient Mesopotamia." *JESHO* 31 (1988) 121-185.

Falkenstein, A. *Archaische Texte aus Uruk* (=*ATU* 1). Berlin 1936.

Friberg, J. *The Early Roots of Babylonian Mathematics I-II*. Göteborg 1978-1979.

Gelb, I. "Methods of Decipherment." *JRAS* 1975, 95-104.

Girshman, R. "Une tablette proto-élamite du plateau iranien." *RA* 31 (1934) 115-119.
_____. *Fouilles de Tépé Sialk I*. Paris 1938.

Green, M. "The Construction and Implementation of the Cuneiform Writing System." *Visible Language* 15 (1981) 345-372.

Hinz, W. "Problems of Linear Elamite," *JRAS* 1975, 106-115.

Johnson, G. *Local Exchange and Early State Development in Southwestern Iran* (=*Anthropological Papers of the Museum of Anthropology, University of Michigan*, no. 51). Ann Arbor 1973.

Lamberg-Karlovsky, C.C. "An Early City in Iran." *Scientific American* 224/6 (June 1971) 102-111.
_____. "Proto-elamite Account Tablets from Tepe Yahya, Iran." *Kadmos* 10 (1971) 97-99.
_____. ""The Proto-elamite Settlement at Tepe Yahya." *Iran* 9 (1971) 87-96.
_____. *Urban Interaction on the Iranian Plateau: Excavations at Tepe Yahya 1967-1973*. Oxford 1974.
_____. "The Third Millennium of Tepe Yahya: A Preliminary Statement." *Proceedings of the IVth Annual Symposium on Archaeological Research in Iran* (Teheran 1976) 71-84.
_____. "The Proto-Elamites on the Iranian Plateau." *Antiquity* 52 (1978) 114-120.
_____. "Further Tracks on the Earliest History of the Iranian Plateau," paper presented to the *Second USSR/USA Archaeological Exchange in the Archaeology of the Ancient Near East, Central Asia, and the Indus*, Samarkand, USSR, 8-22 September 1983. Published in part in the *Information Bulletin of the International Association for the Study of the Cultures of Central Asia* 6. Moscow 1984, 49-53, as "The *longue durée* of the Ancient Near East," in J.-L. Huot et al., eds., *De l'Indus aux Balkans* (=*Fs. Deshayes*). Paris 1985, 55-72, and as "Third Millennium Structure and Process: From the Euphrates to the Indus and the Oxus to the Indian Ocean." *OrAnt.* 25 [1986] 189-219.
_____. "Foreign Relations in the Third Millennium at Tepe Yahya," in *Le plateau iranien et l'Asie centrale des origines à la conquête islamique* (=*Actes du Colloque international du CNRS* no. 567). Paris 1977, 33-43.

Lamberg-Karlovsky, C. C. and M. Tosi. "Shahr-i Sokhta and Tepe Yahya: Tracks on the Earliest History of the Iranian Plateau." *East and West* 23 (1973) 21-57.

Langdon, S. *Pictographic Inscriptions from Jemdet Nasr* (=*OECT* 7). Oxford 1928.

Le Brun, A. "Recherches stratigraphiques à l'Acropole de Suse, 1969-1971." *CahDAFI* 1 (1971) 163-216.
_____. "La glyptique du niveau 17B de l'acropole (campagne de 1972)." *CahDAFI* 8 (1978) 61-79.

Le Brun, A., and Vallat, F. "L'origine de l'écriture à Suse." *CahDAFI* 8 (1978) 11-57.

Mecquenem, R. de. *Epigraphie proto-élamite* (=*MDP* 31). Paris 1949.
_____. "Notes proto-élamites." *RA* 50 (1956) 200-204.

Meriggi, P. "Altsumerische und proto-elamische Bilderschrift." *ZDMG* Spl. 1 (1969) 156-163.
_____. *La scrittura proto-elamica* I-III. Rome 1971-1974.
_____. "Comparaisons des systèmes idéographiques mino-mycénien et proto-élamique," in M. Ruipérez, ed., *Acta Mycenaea* 2 (=*Minos* 12, 1972) 9-17.
_____. "Der Stand der Erforschung des Proto-elamischen." *JRAS* 1975, 105.

Nissen, H. "Grabungen in den Quadraten K/L XII in Uruk-Warka." *BagM* 5 (1970) 136-142.

Picchioni, F. "La direzione della scrittura cuneiforme e gli archivi di Tell Mardikh Ebla." *Or* 49 (1980) 225-251.

Porada, E. "Iranian Art and Archaeology: A Report of the Fifth International Congress, 1968." *Archaeology* 22 (1969) 54-65.

Prickett, M. Man, *Land and Water: Settlement Distribution and the Development of Irrigation Agriculture in the Upper Rud-i Gushk Drainage, Southeastern-Iran.* Ann Arbor 1986.

Scheil, V. *Textes élamites-sémitiques (=MDP* 2). Paris 1900.
_____. *Documents en écriture proto-élamite (=MDP* 6). Paris 1905.
_____. *Textes de comptabilité proto-élamites (=MDP* 17). Paris 1923.
_____. *Textes de comptabilité proto-élamites (=MDP* 26). Paris 1935.

Schmandt-Besserat, D. "An Archaic Recording System and the Origin of Writing." *Syro-Mesopotamian Studies* 1/2 (1977) 31-70.
_____. "Tokens at Susa." *OrAnt.* 25 (1986) 93-125 + pls. IV-X.
_____. "The Origins of Writing." *Written Communication* 3/1 (January 1986) 31-45.

Stolper, M. "Preliminary Report on Texts from Tal-e Malyan, 1971-1974," in F. Bagherzadeh, ed., *Proceedings of the IVth Annual Symposium on Archaeological Research in Iran, 3-8 November 1975* (Teheran 1976) 89-100 + 108-109.
_____. "Inscribed Fragments from Khuzistan." *CahDAFI* 8 (1978) 89-96.
_____. "Proto-elamite Texts from Tall-i Malyan." *Kadmos* 24 (1985) 1-12.

Sumner, W. "Excavations at Tall-i Malyan, 1971-1972." *Iran* 12 (1974) 155-180.
_____. "Excavations at Tall-i Malyan (Anshan) 1974." *Iran* 14 (1976) 103-114 + pls. I-III.

Thureau-Dangin, F. "Tablettes à signes picturaux." *RA* 24 (1927) 23-29.
_____. "Notes assyriologiques LX: Le système décimal chez les anciens Sumériens." *RA* 29 (1932) 22-23.

Tosi, M. "Shahr-i Sokhta." *Iran* 14 (1976) 167-168.

Vaiman, A. "A Comparative Study of the Proto-elamite and Proto- sumerian Scripts" (in Russian). *VDI* 1972:3, 124-133 (English summary p. 133; German translation to appear in *BagM* 20 [1989]).
_____. "The Designation of Male and Female Slaves in the Proto-Sumerian Script" (in Russian). *VDI* 1974:2, 138-148 (German translation to appear in *BagM* 20 [1989]).

Vallat, F. "Les documents épigraphiques de l'Acropole (1969- 1970)." *CahDAFI* 1 (1971) 235-245.
_____. "Les tablettes proto-élamites de l'Acropole (campagne 1972)." *CahDAFI* 3 (1973) 93-107.
_____. "Le matérial épigraphique des couches 18 à 14 de l'Acropole." *Paléorient* 4 (1978) 193-195.
_____. "The Most Ancient Scripts of Iran: The Current Situation." *World Archaeology* 17 (1986) 335-347.

Weiss, H., and Young, T. "The Merchants of Susa." *Iran* 13 (1975) 1-18.

PLATES

Photographs and copies of texts are reproduced 1:1.
In some cases conventional forms of signs have been chosen to facilitate reading of the texts.

TY 1

Obverse   Reverse

TY 2

Obverse   Reverse

TY 3   **TY 4**   **TY 5**

TY 1

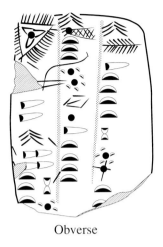

Obverse

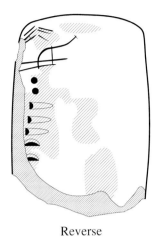

Reverse

TY 2

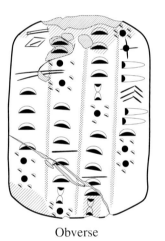

Obverse

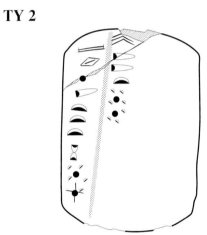

Reverse

TY 3

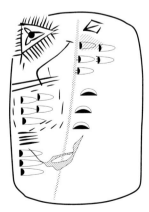

TY 4

TY 5

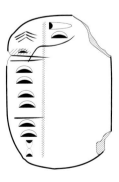

TY 6

TY 7

Obverse   Reverse

TY 8

Obverse   Reverse

TY 9

TY 10

TY 11

TY 6

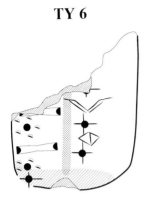

TY 7

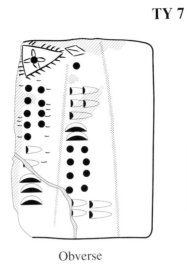

Obverse

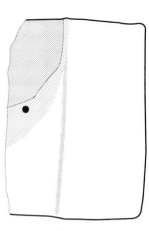

Reverse

TY 8

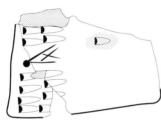

Obverse

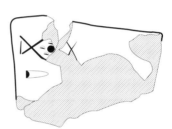

Reverse

TY 9

TY 10

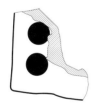

TY 11

TY 12

TY 13

TY 14

TY 15

TY 16

TY 17

TY 12

TY 13

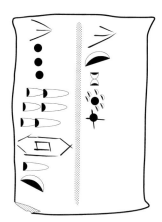

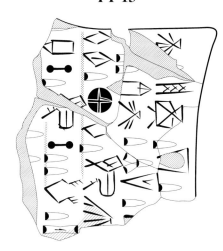

TY 14

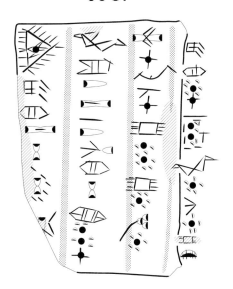

TY 15

TY 16

TY 17

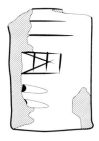

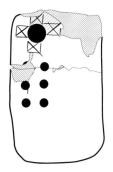

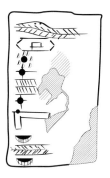

TY 18

Obverse   Reverse

TY 19   **TY 20**

Obverse   Reverse

TY 21

TY 18

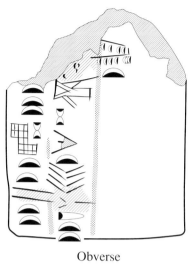

Obverse

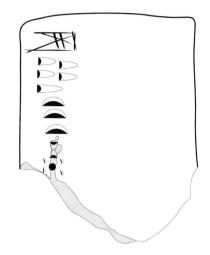

Reverse

TY 19

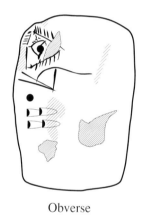

Obverse

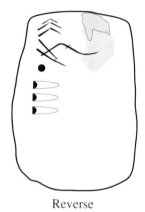

Reverse

TY 20

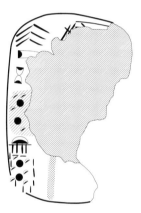

TY 21

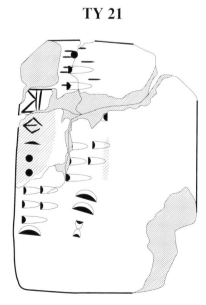

TY 22

TY 23

TY 24

TY 25

TY 26

TY 27

TY 22

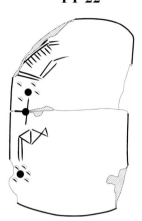

TY 23

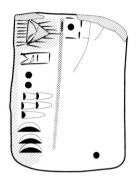

TY 24

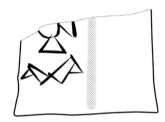

TY 25

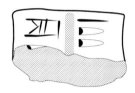

TY 26

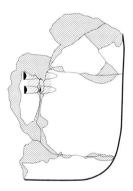

TY 27

PLATE 6

Blank tablets found on the floor of Room 5 (see figure 1).